AUTHOR OF MORE THAN 220 BOOKS
EDWARD D. ANDREWS

ANGELS & DEMONS

THE BIBLE ANSWERS

ANGELS & DEMONS

The Bible Answers

Edward D. Andrews

Christian Publishing House
Cambridge, Ohio

Copyright © 2017 Edward D. Andrews

All rights reserved. Except for brief quotations in articles, other publications, book reviews, and blogs, no part of this book may be reproduced in any manner without prior written permission from the publishers. For information, write, support@christianpublishers.org

Unless otherwise stated, Scripture quotations are from Updated American Standard Version (UASV) Copyright © 2022 by Christian Publishing House

ANGELS & DEMONS: The Bible Answers by Edward D. Andrews

ISBN-13: **978-1-945757-52-5**

ISBN-10: **1-945757-52-3**

Table of Contents

Book Description 6
Preface 7
Introduction 8
CHAPTER 1 Understanding Angels: Their Role, Nature, Abilities, and Interactions 9
CHAPTER 2 Understanding Satan the Devil 17
CHAPTER 3 Explaining the Demons 25
CHAPTER 4 Genesis 6:2 Who were the "sons of God"? .. 27
CHAPTER 5 Genesis 6:2 The Nephilim: Giants of Antiquity 29
CHAPTER 6 Has Anyone Seen God? 31
CHAPTER 7 Who Is Michael the Archangel? 35
CHAPTER 8 Who Is Gabriel? 43
CHAPTER 9 Rebellion in the Spirit Realm 45
CHAPTER 10 The Devil's Influence on Humanity: Can He Control You? 50
CHAPTER 11 Can Satan Read Our Thoughts? 52
CHAPTER 12 Our Struggle against Dark Spiritual Forces 54
CHAPTER 13 The Importance of Learning About Angels 66
CHAPTER 14 Do We Have Our Own Guardian Angels?. 80
CHAPTER 15 Is There a Difference Between Immortality and Eternal Life? 88
CHAPTER 16 The Cosmic Conflict: Truth vs. Lies 91
GLOSSARY of Related Biblical Terms 108

Edward D. Andrews

Book Description

In the realm of spiritual beliefs, few topics captivate the imagination as profoundly as angels and demons. From the highest heavens to the depths of the abyss, these spirit beings have fascinated and intrigued humanity for millennia. But what does the Bible, the cornerstone of Christian faith, truly reveal about these powerful entities?

In "ANGELS & DEMONS: The Bible Answers," delve deep into Scripture's pages to discover the genuine nature, roles, and significance of these celestial and malevolent beings. Drawing from a conservative Biblical viewpoint, this comprehensive guide illuminates the divine purpose of angels, the sinister plots of demons, and the profound impact both have on the human story.

Starting with a foundational exploration of angels and their divine functions, the book segues into a deep dive into the enigmatic figure of Satan the Devil. The narrative then expands into the complex nature of demons and their historical interplay with humankind. Intriguing subjects such as the mysterious "sons of God" from Genesis, the Nephilim, and the identities of archangels Michael and Gabriel are tackled with scholarly precision.

Beyond mere definitions and accounts, this book also delves into pivotal questions about spiritual warfare, Satan's influence on humanity, and the distinctions between eternal life and immortality. Each chapter offers both enlightening details and profound insights, equipping readers with the Biblical answers they seek.

Whether you're a student of theology, a curious soul, or someone seeking clarity on spiritual entities, "ANGELS & DEMONS: The Bible Answers" stands as an essential guidebook. Journey through the pages, and arm yourself with the timeless truths that have been meticulously extracted from God's inspired Word. This volume not only answers your most pressing questions but also fortifies your faith in the face of spiritual battles.

Preface

Throughout human history, the ethereal and the supernatural have occupied a central place in our collective psyche. Legends and tales, stories of old and new, all converge upon the profound influence of angels and demons. Their stories are not just allegories or fables but a testament to the age-old struggle between good and evil, light and darkness.

As a conservative Bible scholar, my journey into the heart of Scriptures has been driven by a deep passion to understand these spiritual entities beyond the lore and myths that often surround them. The Bible, with its rich tapestry of narratives and teachings, provides a unique and authoritative perspective on angels and demons, challenging preconceived notions and reshaping our understanding.

This book is a culmination of years of study, reflection, and prayerful contemplation. The chapters within are more than just explanations; they are an invitation. An invitation to dive deeper into the Word of God, to question, to seek, and ultimately, to understand. In a world where misinformation abounds, and where the lines between fact and fiction often blur, I hope this work serves as a lighthouse, guiding readers towards the truth, and illuminating the path of understanding.

As you turn these pages, may you embark on a transformative journey, one that strengthens your faith, enriches your knowledge, and prepares you for the spiritual battles that lie ahead. This is not just a book; it is a spiritual adventure, one I am honored to share with you.

Edward D. Andrews

Author of 220+ books and Chief Translator of the Updated American Standard Version

Edward D. Andrews

Introduction

Every culture, every civilization, every heart, at some point, grapples with the questions that lie just beyond the veil of our physical world. What are these spiritual entities we've come to identify as angels and demons? Where did they originate, and how do they influence the ebb and flow of our earthly journey? Our stories, films, art, and even our night-time musings have been painted with vivid images of these mysterious beings, both benevolent and malevolent.

The Bible, that ancient collection of books revered by billions, doesn't leave us in the dark on these topics. Yet, many who delve into its pages seeking answers about angels and demons emerge with a myriad of interpretations and, at times, more questions than they began with. The intent of this work is to streamline this vast biblical information, drawing from the Scriptures themselves to provide a clear, concise, and coherent picture of the roles and realities of angels and demons.

Beyond merely a scholarly endeavor, this book aims to equip its readers with the spiritual discernment needed in an age of skepticism and sensationalism. We will travel back to the dawn of time, retracing the footsteps of these spiritual entities, understanding their decisions, their conflicts, and their interactions with humanity. This journey is more than just uncovering knowledge; it's about understanding the greater narrative of God's divine plan and our place within it.

So, with an open heart and a keen mind, let us set forth on this exploration, trusting that the Word of God will light our path, and its truths will set us free.

CHAPTER 1 Understanding Angels: Their Role, Nature, Abilities, and Interactions

The terms "messenger" in both Hebrew (*mal·'akh'*) and Greek (*ag'ge·los*) appear nearly 400 times throughout the Bible. These words can be translated as "angels" when referring to spirit messengers. However, when clearly referring to humans, they are translated as "messengers." (Ge 16:7; 32:3; Jas 2:25; Re 22:8) Notably, in the symbolic writings of Revelation, some references to 'angels' could also mean human beings.—Re 2:1, 8, 12, 18; 3:1, 7, 14.

Context is crucial in discerning whether these "messengers" are human or angelic. Isaiah 63:9 provides an example: Jehovah's "personal messenger" in this case is likely an angel since the messenger saved the Israelites. (Compare Ex 14:19, 20.)

Describing Angels

Often, angels are referred to as spirits. Being spirit denotes invisibility and power, such as when scriptures say: "A spirit came out and stood before Jehovah." (1Ki 22:21; Heb 1:14) As they have spiritual bodies, angels reside "in the heavens." (Mr 12:25; 1Co 15:44, 50) They're also described as "sons of the true God," "morning stars," and "holy myriads."—Job 1:6; 2:1; 38:7; De 33:2.

Since angels don't marry or reproduce, they were each individually crafted by Jehovah through his premier Son, known as "the beginning of the creation by God." (Mt 22:30; Re 3:14) This principal Son, often referred to as the Word, was the means by which all other angels came into existence long before mankind. This is evident from scriptures that speak of angels rejoicing during Earth's creation.—Job 38:4-7.

In terms of their sheer number, the book of Daniel speaks of "a thousand thousands that kept ministering to [God], and ten thousand times ten thousand that kept standing right before him."—Da 7:10; Heb 12:22; Jude 14.

Hierarchy Among Angels

The angelic realm, like the visible universe, operates with a hierarchy. The leading angel in terms of authority and might is Michael, the archangel. (Da 10:13, 21; 12:1; Jude 9; Re 12:7) Other high-ranking angels include the seraphs (Isa 6:2, 6) and the cherubs, who have special roles and are mentioned around 90 times in the Scriptures. (Ge 3:24; Eze 10:1-22) Then there's the vast majority of angelic beings, who, beyond just relaying messages, act as God's agents, executing His will - from the protection of His people to the annihilation of wicked ones.—Ge 19:1-26.

Individual Personalities of Angels

While some argue that angels are just impersonal forces used by God, the Bible presents a different picture. The fact that we know the names of certain angels, like Michael and Gabriel, shows that they have distinct personalities. (Da 12:1; Lu 1:26) The limited naming is likely to prevent us from giving these beings excessive honor, which they themselves wouldn't seek. Remember, angels act on behalf of God, not on their own behalf. When individuals in the Bible asked angels for their names, they often refrained from revealing them. (Ge 32:29; Jos 5:14; Jg 13:17, 18) Twice, the apostle John was warned against worshiping angels, being told to worship only God.—Re 19:10; 22:8, 9.

Angels have the capacity for communication (1Co 13:1), knowledge of various human languages (Nu 22:32-35; Da 4:23; Ac 10:3-7), and the ability to praise Jehovah (Ps 148:2; Lu 2:13). Though they are sexless by God's design, they are typically represented as male. However, some materialized as males and acted against God's design, leading to their expulsion from heaven. Like humans, they have free will, choosing right from wrong. Some chose to follow Satan in his rebellion.—Re 12:7-9; Mt 25:41.

Powers and Limitations

Angels, being created above humans (Heb 2:7), possess superior mental capabilities and power. They are described as "mighty in power" (Ps 103:20) and have demonstrated immense might, as seen when two angels devastated Sodom and Gomorrah or when one angel slew 185,000 Assyrian soldiers overnight (Ge 19:13, 24; 2Ki 19:35).

They can move incredibly swiftly, surpassing physical boundaries. This is evident when an angel reached Daniel almost immediately after God sent him in response to Daniel's prayer.—Da 9:20-23.

However, despite their heightened abilities, angels are not omniscient. They did not know when the current world order would end (Mt 24:36), and there are aspects of God's plan they don't fully grasp (1Pe 1:12). Still, they express joy at a sinner's repentance, keenly observe Christians' activities, and appreciate symbolic gestures like the sign of authority worn by Christian women.—Lu 15:10; 1Co 4:9; 11:10.

Role in Biblical Events

Throughout history, angels have played key roles in executing God's plans. They've aided numerous Bible figures like Abraham, Moses, Peter, and Paul. (Ge 22:11; Ac 5:19, 20; 7:35; 12:7, 8) They've also directly contributed to the Bible's content, with the book of Revelation featuring them prominently. In Revelation, multitudes of angels surround Jehovah's throne, and angels play vital roles in the events described, such as sounding trumpets, delivering messages, and executing divine judgments.—Re 5:11; 7:11; 8:6; 14:6, 8; 16:1.

Edward D. Andrews

The Role of Angels in Christ's Journey and Their Support for Believers

Angels with Jesus

Throughout Jesus' life on earth, angels played pivotal roles. They heralded His conception, announced His birth, and were by His side after His 40-day fasting period. In Gethsemane, during His intense prayer, an angel came to strengthen Him. When confronted by a mob, Jesus mentioned He could summon more than 12 legions of angels if He wished. These celestial beings didn't stop there. They announced His resurrection and bore witness to His ascension into heaven.—Mt 4:11; 26:53; 28:5-7; Lu 1:30, 31; 2:10, 11; 22:43; Ac 1:10, 11.

Angels and Followers of Christ

Following Jesus' ascent, angels continued their services to His followers, aligning with Jesus' promise: "Do not despise one of these little ones; for I tell you that their angels in heaven always behold the face of my Father." (Mt 18:10) They are described as "spirits for public service" dedicated to those set to inherit salvation. (Heb 1:14) While these divine messengers no longer make visible appearances like when they freed apostles from prison, they remain a protective, unseen presence, akin to the protective forces surrounding the prophet Elisha. As the Psalms declare, God commands His angels to guard believers, and they encamp around those who fear Him, delivering them from peril.—Ps 91:11; 34:7; Ac 5:19; 2Ki 6:15-17.

Angels in Judgment and War

Scripture also depicts angels accompanying Jesus during judgment times, aiding in distinguishing "the wheat" from "the weeds" and "the sheep" from "the goats." They sided with Michael in the celestial battle against the dragon and its minions upon the establishment of God's Kingdom in heaven. Moreover, they'll be by the side of the King of kings in the monumental battle known as the great day of God the Almighty.—Mt 13:41; 25:31-33; Re 12:7-10; 19:14-16.

Understanding Seraphs

Seraphs are spiritual entities stationed around Jehovah's heavenly throne. The term "seraphim" in Hebrew essentially means "burning ones." This word takes its root from "sa·raph'", implying "burn." At other times, the term refers to earthly creatures, indicating "poisonous" or "fiery snake."—Nu 21:6, 8, ftns.

Isaiah's Vision In Isaiah's profound vision, he describes:

Isaiah 6:1-7 Updated American Standard Version (UASV)

6 In the year that King Uzziah died I saw Jehovah sitting upon a throne, high and lifted up; and the train of his robe filled the temple. ² Above him stood the seraphim. Each had six wings: with two he covered his face, and with two he covered his feet, and with two he flew. ³ And one called to another and said:

"Holy, holy, holy is Jehovah of armies;¹ the whole earth is full of his glory!"

⁴ And the foundations of the thresholds shook at the voice of him who called, and the house was filled with smoke. ⁵ And I said: "Woe is me! For I have been brought to silence; for I am a man of unclean lips, and I dwell in the midst of a people of unclean lips; for my eyes have seen the King, Jehovah of armies!"

⁶ Then one of the seraphim flew to me, having in his hand a burning coal that he had taken with tongs from the altar. ⁷ And he

---

¹ **Jehovah of armies:** (יְהוָה צְבָאוֹת Jehovah tsebaot) literally means an army of soldiers or military forces (Gen. 21:22; Deut. 20:9). The expression is found 285 times, with some deviations, in the Scriptures. The prophetic books, especially Isaiah, Jeremiah, and Zechariah, have the most occurrences. It is also used figuratively, "the sun and the moon and the stars, all the armies of heaven." (Deut. 4:19) In the plural form, it is also used of the Israelites forces as well. (Ex. 6:26; 7:4; Num. 33:1; Psa. 44:9) However, the "armies" in the expression "Jehovah of armies" is a reference to the angelic forces primarily, if not exclusively. Paul and James, quoting from the Old Testament prophecies, used its equivalent (τὰ κυρίου σαβαὼθ ta kuriou sabaōth; "the Lord of armies") in their writings.—Rom. 9:29; Jas 5:4; cf. Isa 1:9.

touched my mouth and said: "Look, this has touched your lips; your guilt is taken away, and your sin atoned for."

While Jehovah's divine form isn't explicitly described, his magnificence is evident as even the hem of his robe filled the temple, and his throne was elevated.

Their Status

Seraphs, as angels, hold a significant position in God's celestial hierarchy, evident by their proximity to God's throne. Their high rank aligns with the cherubs seen in Ezekiel's vision escorting God's divine chariot. These varying heavenly ranks align with Colossians 1:16, which touches on various roles in the heavens.

Role and Responsibilities

The number of seraphs isn't specified, but their chants suggest they were spread out on both sides of the throne, echoing each other's proclamations of Jehovah's holiness and magnificence. Displaying humility, they covered their faces and feet with two of their wing sets, paying respect to the Heavenly King.

The seraphs' declaration about God's holiness implies their duty to ensure His holiness and glory are acknowledged universally. One seraph symbolically cleansed Isaiah of his sins using a glowing coal, suggesting that they might have roles related to purification based on Jesus Christ's sacrifice.

Symbolic Representation

Their described form, having feet, wings, and other features, is symbolic. These features likely represent their capabilities or duties. It aligns with how God often symbolically represents Himself with human-like attributes. As the apostle John notes, God's true form remains a mystery; when He reveals Himself, believers will witness His true self.—1Jo 3:2.

Understanding Cherubs

A cherub is a high-ranking angelic being with specific responsibilities, distinct from seraphs. Their first biblical mention is in Genesis 3:24. After Adam and Eve's expulsion from Eden, cherubs guarded the eastern entrance to the tree of life. The exact number stationed there remains unspecified.

Cherubs in the Tabernacle

Cherubic figures adorned the wilderness tabernacle's furnishings. Two gold cherubs, facing each other with wings spread protectively over the Ark's cover, symbolized reverence and guardianship. Moreover, tent cloths for the tabernacle and the dividing curtain between the Holy and Most Holy had embroidered cherub patterns. Contrary to some claims, these weren't grotesque figures resembling pagan idols. Traditional Jewish beliefs (though not explicitly stated in the Bible) suggest these cherubs had human forms. These artistically detailed representations were crafted according to the divine pattern shown to Moses, portraying angels of breathtaking beauty. These cherubs symbolized Jehovah's presence, making it appear as though Jehovah was "sitting upon the cherubs." They also figuratively served as Jehovah's celestial chariot, providing both protection and swift transportation. David lyrically depicted Jehovah's rapid assistance, describing Him as flying on a cherub's wings.

Cherubs in Solomon's Temple

Solomon's temple blueprint included two grand cherubs in the Most Holy. These 14.6-foot-tall cherubs, made of gold-covered wood, stood with wings touching, guarding the Ark of the Covenant. Their designs also decorated the temple walls, doors, and even copper water carriages. Similarly, Ezekiel's envisioned temple was adorned with cherub carvings.

In Ezekiel's visions, he saw symbolic cherubs with unique attributes, often accompanying Jehovah's radiant figure. These cherubs represented unwavering devotion to Jehovah.

Lastly, in Ezekiel's prophetic book, the "king of Tyre" is metaphorically described as a cherub in Eden. He was portrayed as a once glorious protector, later condemned and cast down for his unrighteousness.—Eze 28:11-19.

CHAPTER 2 Understanding Satan the Devil

Definition and Context

The term "Satan" means "Resister." In the Hebrew Scriptures, the word sa·tan′ often appears without a definite article and refers to any opponent or adversary. For example, it describes an angel who opposed Balaam during his mission to curse the Israelites (Nu 22:22, 32). It can also describe humans opposing other humans (1Sa 29:4; 2Sa 19:21, 22; 1Ki 5:4; 11:14, 23, 25). However, when paired with the definite article ha, it refers to Satan the Devil, God's primary Adversary (Job 1:6, ftn; 2:1-7; Zec 3:1, 2). The Greek Scriptures use the word sa·ta·nas′ to mostly refer to Satan the Devil, typically with the definite article ho.

Origin and Transition to Evil

Satan wasn't always known by this name. This title was given due to his resistance and opposition to God. His original name remains undisclosed. Being a creation of God, he was originally a perfect, righteous spirit being. This is evident from his appearances in heaven before God (Job chaps 1, 2; Re 12:9). Jesus revealed that Satan deviated from truth, leading to sin: "That one was a manslayer when he began, and he did not stand fast in the truth, because truth is not in him." (John 8:44; 1Jo 3:8). Jesus indicates that Satan left his righteous state and initiated the path of sin, leading to mankind's downfall by deceiving Adam and Eve. This act brought death to humans (Ro 5:12). His attributes and actions throughout the Scriptures confirm his existence as a person, not merely a concept of evil.

From being a righteous spirit, Satan's own desires led him into sin. This transformation mirrors James' description of how desire can lead to sin and, ultimately, to death (Jas 1:14, 15). Ezekiel 28:11-19, while describing the king of Tyre, may offer a parallel to Satan's own downfall.

Satan's deception of Eve through a serpent is a pivotal event in the Scriptures. This act earned him titles such as "Serpent," symbolizing deception, "the Tempter," and "the father of the lie" (Ge 3:1-7; 2Co 11:3; Mt 4:3; John 8:44; Re 12:9).

Understanding Satan's Challenge to God's Sovereignty

The Temptation of Eve

When Satan, speaking through a serpent, approached Eve, he directly questioned Jehovah's rightful rule and honesty. Satan implied that God was unfairly keeping something from Eve. He declared that God lied about the consequences of eating the forbidden fruit. Moreover, Satan convinced her that by eating the fruit, she would become as powerful and knowledgeable as God. Through these deceptions, Satan positioned himself above God in Eve's perspective, effectively becoming a god to her. As a result, humanity came under Satan's influence, setting him as a rival to Jehovah.—Ge 3:1-7.

Satan's Bold Challenge in Heaven

The Bible provides insight into heavenly events, showing Satan boldly challenging Jehovah. He believed he could sway Job, one of God's loyal servants. Satan insinuated that Job's loyalty to God was due to selfish reasons and that, if tested, Job's true nature would be exposed as corrupt. Satan emphasized this by saying, "Skin in behalf of skin, and everything that a man has he will give in behalf of his soul. For a change, thrust out your hand, please, and touch as far as his bone and his flesh and see whether he will not curse you to your very face." —Job 1:6-12; 2:1-7.

In this instance, God permitted Satan to test Job's integrity. Satan demonstrated his power and malevolence through a series of calamities on Job and his family. But notably, when God commanded him not to take Job's life, Satan complied, acknowledging his limitations before God's ultimate authority.—Job 2:6.

The Title "Devil"

Satan's actions, from challenging God to accusing God's servants, earned him the title "Devil," which means "Slanderer." This was especially after his deceitful act in the garden of Eden.

Satan's Allies: The Fallen Angels

Before Noah's Flood, some of God's angels left their heavenly realm and positions. They took human form, married women, and produced the Nephilim. By deserting God, these angels aligned with Satan, making him "the ruler of the demons." Once, when Jesus expelled demons from a person, some accused him of using the power of "Beelzebub, the ruler of the demons." Jesus' response indicated they were referring to Satan: "If Satan expels Satan, he has become divided against himself."—Mt 12:22-27.

Satan's Dominance Over Earth

The apostle Paul describes Satan as a powerful force, associating him with "the wicked spirit forces in the heavenly places" and the "world rulers of this darkness." As the ruler of this unseen realm surrounding the earth, he is "the ruler of the authority of the air." He's shown to deceive the world and is hence termed "the ruler of this world." Aligning with the world means aligning with Satan, highlighting the gravity of James' warning that "the friendship with the world is enmity with God."—Jas 4:4.

Satan's Attempt to Eliminate the "Seed"

Early on, Satan sought to disrupt the promise of the "seed" that was to emerge from Abraham. (Ge 12:7) He apparently plotted to defile Sarah, hoping to make her unworthy of bearing the seed. However, Jehovah safeguarded her. (Ge 20:1-18) Throughout biblical history, Satan persistently targeted Abraham's descendants, the Israelites, tempting them into sin and pitting other nations against them. Satan's endeavors against God seemingly peaked when Babylon, the Third World Power in biblical times, conquered Jerusalem. They overthrew King Zedekiah from David's lineage, demolished Jehovah's temple, and left Jerusalem and Judah desolate.—Eze 21:25-27.

Under Satan's influence, the royal line of Babylon, inaugurated by Nebuchadnezzar, imprisoned Israel for 68 years until their eventual downfall. Babylon had no plans of freeing their captives, echoing Satan's own ambitious stand against Jehovah, the Universal Sovereign. The Babylonian monarchs, devout followers of deities like Marduk and Ishtar, essentially bowed to demons, falling under Satan's control given their detachment from Jehovah.—Ps 96:5; 1Co 10:20; Eph 2:12; Col 1:21.

Driven by Satan, the Babylonian king yearned to reign supreme, dreaming of dominance over "Jehovah's throne" (1Ch 29:23) and the "stars of God," referring to the lineage of Davidic kings. This Babylonian dynasty viewed itself as the "shining one," or the "son of the dawn." Some translations maintain the term "Lucifer," which is essentially the Latin Vulgate's interpretation of the Hebrew word heh·lel', denoting "shining one." This term isn't a name or title but signifies the proud stance of Babylon's kings. (Isa 14:4-21) Since Satan manipulated Babylon, its ruler mirrored Satan's own overreaching desires. However, Jehovah once again rescued His people by restoring them to their homeland, in anticipation of the foretold Seed.—Ezr 1:1-6.

Satan's Attempts to Challenge Jesus

Recognizing Jesus as God's Son and the prophesied one to challenge him (Ge 3:15), Satan tried repeatedly to destroy Jesus. However, the angel Gabriel, while announcing Jesus' conception to

Mary, reassured her, stating: "The Holy Spirit will come upon you, and power of the Most High will overshadow you. Hence, what is born will be called holy, God's Son." (Lu 1:35) God's protection was evident, especially when plots to end Jesus' life as a baby failed. (Mt 2:1-15) As Jesus matured, God continued shielding him.

Post baptism, Jesus faced Satan's three-fold temptations in the wilderness, testing his loyalty to Jehovah. Satan even showcased all global kingdoms, asserting they were his dominion. Jesus neither accepted this claim nor any shortcuts to power, responding, "Be gone, Satan! For it is written, 'You shall worship the Lord your God and him only shall you serve.'" Following this, Satan retreated, waiting for a more opportune moment (Mt 4:1-11; Lu 4:13). This affirms James' assertion: "Oppose the Devil, and he will flee from you."—Jas 4:7.

Jesus was consistently aware of Satan's schemes, including temptations to divert from Jehovah's will. This became evident when Peter, despite his noble intentions, inadvertently tempted Jesus. When Jesus hinted at his impending sufferings, Peter rebuked him. Jesus responded sharply, "Get behind me, Satan! You are a hindrance to me. For you are not setting your mind on the things of God, but on the things of man.'"—Mt 16:21-23.

Throughout his mission, Jesus faced dangers. Satan manipulated individuals to either thwart or assassinate him. At a point, people tried making Jesus their king, but he awaited God's designated time for such a role (John 6:15). His hometown citizens even attempted his murder (Lu 4:22-30), and many sought to ensnare him (Mt 22:15). Yet, Satan could never make Jesus waver in thought or action. As Jesus declared near his end: "Now the ruler of this world will be cast out"— thoroughly debunked. (John 12:31) Although mankind was under Satan's sin-induced grip, Jesus confidently stated as his death approached: "The ruler of the world is coming. And he has no hold on me."—John 14:30.

Eventually, Satan influenced Jesus' crucifixion, manipulating one of Jesus' disciples and using both Jewish and Roman authorities to execute him painfully (Lu 22:3; Joh 13:26, 27; chaps 18, 19). Acting as "the one having the means to cause death, that is, the Devil," (Heb

2:14; Lu 22:53) Satan's actions fulfilled prophecies about Jesus' sacrificial death. This death, owing to Jesus' purity, offered humanity's ransom. His death (and God-led resurrection) enabled Jesus to free mankind from Satan's clutches, as noted, "he might bring to nothing the one having the means to cause death, that is, the Devil; and emancipate all those fearing death, enslaved throughout their lives."—Heb 2:14, 15.

Satan's Relentless Battle Against Christians

Even after Jesus' resurrection, Satan persisted in his aggressive campaign against Christ's followers. The narratives in the book of Acts and letters from the Christian Greek Scriptures provide ample evidence of this. Paul mentioned being tormented by "a thorn in the flesh, an angel of Satan." (2Co 12:7) Much like with Eve, Satan masked his true intentions by "transforming himself into an angel of light." He even had deceptive agents who "keep transforming themselves into ministers of righteousness." (2Co 11:14, 15) Such deceivers included the fake apostles who opposed Paul (2Co 11:13) and those in Smyrna who falsely claimed Jewish heritage, described as a "synagogue of Satan." (Re 2:9) Satan didn't halt his "day and night" accusations against Christians, continually questioning their faithfulness, mirroring his challenge to Job's integrity. (Re 12:10; Lu 22:31) Nevertheless, Christians had an advocate: "a helper with the Father, Jesus Christ, a righteous one," representing them before God.—1Jo 2:1.

The Demise and Ultimate End of Satan

When Satan instigated Eve's rebellion against God, and subsequently Adam's, God addressed the serpent (directly referring to Satan as a mere animal wouldn't comprehend the depth of the matter): "Dust is what you will eat all the days of your life. And I shall put enmity between you and the woman and between your seed and her seed. He will bruise you in the head and you will bruise him in the heel." (Ge 3:14, 15) Here, God foretold Satan's eventual fate, hinting at his inevitable downfall. The "seed" would deal Satan a fatal blow. The demons recognized Christ as the one destined to confine them to the "abyss," an apparent state of restriction akin to "torment."—Mt 8:29; Lu 8:30, 31.

The book of Revelation outlines Satan's final days. When Christ seizes kingdom authority, Satan is cast from heaven to earth, losing his heavenly access. (Re 12:7-12) Following this expulsion, he's granted a "short period of time" to battle "the remaining ones of [the woman's] seed," who remain loyal to God. As the "dragon," Satan seeks to crush these faithful ones. (Re 12:16, 17)

Revelation 20 depicts Satan's confinement for a millennium, bound by a mighty angel, likely Jesus Christ. After Christ's thousand-year reign, Satan, briefly released, makes a last-ditch effort against God's sovereignty, only to face eternal destruction alongside his demons in the lake of fire and sulfur.—Re 20:1-3, 7-10.

Understanding the Concept of 'Handing Over to Satan'

When addressing the situation in the Corinthian congregation where a member was engaging in a scandalous relationship with his stepmother, the apostle Paul stated, "Hand such a man over to Satan for the destruction of the flesh." (1Co 5:5) Paul was instructing the congregation to expel this individual, severing all ties with him. (1Co 5:13) By doing this, the man would be removed from the congregation and thrust into the world, a realm where Satan holds influence. This action is analogous to removing "a little leaven" from dough to prevent it from affecting the whole. By expelling this man, the congregation was purifying itself from corrupt influence. (1Co 5:6, 7) Paul used a similar approach with Hymenaeus and Alexander, who had deviated from their faith.—1Ti 1:20.

Later on, it seems that the aforementioned man from Corinth showed genuine remorse and mended his ways. Paul then advised the congregation to welcome him back. Stressing the importance of forgiveness, Paul mentioned, "that we may not be overreached by Satan, for we are not ignorant of his designs." (2Co 2:11) Initially, the congregation was reprimanded by Paul for their complacency towards the man's sinful behavior, even displaying arrogance by tolerating it. (1Co 5:2) However, Paul cautioned them against being too rigid now; if they denied forgiveness to the repentant man, they would fall into another of Satan's traps by becoming uncompassionate. Christians are guided by God's Word to recognize Satan's tactics, enabling them to counteract his maneuvers using the spiritual tools that God offers.—Eph 6:13-17.

CHAPTER 3 Explaining the Demons

A demon is an **invisible, malevolent, spirit being** with powers beyond human abilities. The word from the Greek Scriptures often used for demon is dai·mo′ni·on. The term "spirit" (Pneu′ma in Greek) can also refer to these wicked spirits. At times, this term is combined with other descriptors like "wicked," "unclean," "mute," and "deaf."

Origin and Activities

These demons were not directly created by God. The first to become a demon was Satan, who then led other angels astray, making them demons too. During Noah's time, these disobedient angels took physical forms, married human women, and produced offspring called the Nephilim. When the Flood came, these angels returned to the spirit realm but lost their former status. They were restrained, left in a condition of spiritual darkness, unable to take physical form again but still capable of influencing humans and even possessing them. This includes using objects like houses and charms. Their primary goal is to divert humans away from pure worship of Jehovah.

In Jesus' time, demon activity was widespread. Many of Jesus' miracles involved expelling these wicked spirits from people. He also empowered his apostles and disciples to do the same. Demonic influence remains strong today, and Scripture warns of an increase in their activities as the end approaches.

Defending Against Demons

Christians must actively resist these unseen malevolent forces. They need to be vigilant because even the demons acknowledge God and tremble at His power. Some might be deceived by demonic teachings in the future. One cannot serve Jehovah and still engage with demons. Thus, believers must stand firm against these dark forces.

Demons in Ancient Greek Thought

The understanding of "demon" in the Bible is different from ancient Greek beliefs. In Greek thought, the term had a broader meaning, sometimes referring to divine interventions, both good and evil. When Paul interacted with the Greeks, there were times he had to address their understanding of demons. For instance, when in Athens, Paul noted their deep religious beliefs, which might be termed as superstition by some. When speaking to King Herod Agrippa II, the term was also used to describe the Jews' religious practices.

CHAPTER 4 Genesis 6:2 Who were the "sons of God"?

The term "Sons of the True God" first appears in Genesis 6:2-4. Here, these "sons" are described as being drawn to human women, marrying them before the global Flood.

Human Interpretation

Many believe these "sons of God" were from Seth's lineage, marrying women from Cain's lineage. They suggest this because Noah, a godly man, descended from Seth, while other lines from Adam were wiped out in the Flood. This theory proposes that the marriages between Sethites and Cainites led to the birth of "mighty ones."

However, there isn't solid Scriptural evidence to support this idea. While "sons of men" often has a negative connotation, it's not always used unfavorably.

Angelic Interpretation

Conversely, another perspective is supported by additional Scriptural references. "Sons of the True God" appears in Job 1:6, referring to spirit sons in God's presence. These angelic beings are again mentioned in Job 38:4-7, where they are present during the earth's creation, and in Psalm 89:6, distinguishing them as heavenly.

Some argue this angelic interpretation doesn't fit the context of Genesis 6, which speaks of human wickedness. But if these spirit creatures were involved in human affairs, it could explain the extreme wickedness on earth. Instances in the New Testament, like demonic possession during Jesus' time, show that wicked spirits influenced severe human misconduct.

Further evidence can be found in Peter's letters referencing disobedient spirits during Noah's time (1Pe 3:19, 20) and in Jude's mention of angels that abandoned their rightful place (Jude 6). If the "sons of God" were not angelic, these passages would remain unexplained.

Angels are known to take on human forms, as seen in Genesis where they ate and drank with men. While angels don't marry each other in heaven (Mt 22:30), it doesn't rule out the possibility of them taking human form and marrying human women. The Scriptural evidence, particularly in Jude's letter comparing angels' actions with the sins of Sodom and Gomorrah, suggests these angels acted against their nature during Noah's time.

In conclusion, the strongest Scriptural evidence supports the belief that the "sons of God" in Genesis 6:2-4 were angelic beings.

CHAPTER 5 Genesis 6:2 The Nephilim: Giants of Antiquity

The term "Nephilim" originates from the Hebrew word nephi·lim′, which can be understood to mean "Fellers" or "Those Who Cause [Others] to Fall Down." This term finds its root in the Hebrew verb na·phal′, which signifies "fall." The Nephilim are discussed in the context of Jehovah's dissatisfaction with humanity in the days leading up to Noah's Flood, and they are described in relation to the "sons of the true God" and their interactions with human women. This raises questions about their identity and nature.

Understanding the Nephilim's Identity

There have been numerous interpretations and theories regarding the true identity of the Nephilim.

1. **Human Lineage Theory:** Some theologians and scholars believe that the Nephilim were simply descendants of Seth who intermarried with descendants of Cain. However, the Scriptural evidence does not firmly support this claim.

2. **Angelic Offspring Theory:** Another perspective, supported by multiple scriptures, suggests that these "sons of God" were actually angels. This interpretation posits that these angels rebelled against their heavenly duties, took human form, and bore offspring with human women. This resulted in the creation of the Nephilim, who were hybrids of angels and humans. Such rebellious angels are alluded to in 1 Peter 3:19-20 and Jude 6.

3. **Giants Theory:** Another theory, supported by certain translations, identifies the Nephilim with the "mighty ones" or gib·bo·rim′. This viewpoint is based on the translations that

use the term "giants" to describe both "Nephilim" and "mighty ones."

Analyzing the scriptural context, it is clear that the Nephilim, whether human or hybrid, contributed to the heightened wickedness that precipitated the Great Flood.

The Role of Angels

It is worth noting the potential involvement of angels in the creation of the Nephilim. Angels have the ability to take human form, as demonstrated in various biblical accounts. However, it would be a perversion for them to forsake their spiritual duties to form relationships with humans. The consequences of such rebellious actions by angels are evident in the scriptures that refer to these beings as "spirits in prison" or bound in "Tartarus."

Impacts of the Nephilim's Presence

The presence of these "mighty ones" likely exacerbated the wickedness on Earth. Their existence and the resulting tales may have inspired various mythologies found among ancient civilizations after the Babel dispersion. For instance, many ancient myths from various cultures, including the Greeks, contain stories of gods interacting with humans to produce superhuman heroes or demigods.

Nephilim in Later References

The term "Nephilim" surfaces again in the account of the spies sent by Moses to scout Canaan. These spies gave a fearful report, claiming they saw Nephilim and felt like mere "grasshoppers" in comparison. While there might have been large individuals in Canaan, this report is the sole instance where they are labeled as Nephilim, suggesting the term might have been used for its intimidation value.

CHAPTER 6 Has Anyone Seen God?

Abraham's Experience

The Bible recounts an instance when Abraham, often referred to as "God's friend," was visited by three strangers. He addressed one of them as Jehovah. This brings forth the question: Did Abraham actually see God face to face?

In Genesis 18:1-3, we read: "And Jehovah appeared to him by the oaks of Mamre, as he was sitting at the tent door in the heat of the day. He lifted up his eyes and looked, and behold, three men were standing in front of him. When he saw them, he ran from the entrance of the tent to meet them, and he bowed down to the ground. And he said, 'Jehovah, if I have found favor in your sight, do not pass by your servant.'"

Despite this account, some argue that since Jesus and God are distinct entities, seeing one does not mean seeing the other. But if that's the case, whom did Abraham see?

Jesus' Perspective

Jesus Christ clearly identified himself as the "Son of God," separate from God. He consistently pointed out his relationship as a distinct entity who sought to do the will of his Heavenly Father. (John 10:36; John 5:30) Jesus' expressions during his time on the torture stake and after his resurrection further emphasize his distinction from God.

John, a close apostle of Jesus, asserted that no human has seen God. (John 1:18) This statement challenges the assertion that Abraham saw God in physical form.

Moses' Encounter

Moses, a key biblical figure, expressed a desire to see God. However, Jehovah explained to Moses that he could not see God's face and live. Instead, Moses was allowed to see only God's "back" or afterglow after God's glory passed by. (Exodus 33:18-23)

The Bible speaks of Moses communicating with God "face to face," but this should not be taken literally. This phrase indicates a direct, personal communication between Moses and God, not a physical viewing. (Exodus 33:11) In other biblical passages, it is explained that Moses' experiences with Jehovah were more direct than those of other prophets. They did not involve dreams or visions. However, when Moses saw the "appearance of Jehovah," it was through a vision, not a physical encounter. (Exodus 24:10-11)

The Bible presents a consistent message that no human has seen God in his true form. While there were instances, like with Abraham and Moses, where God's presence was felt or manifested in some manner, these did not involve a direct viewing of God himself. Instead, they were special manifestations or visions provided by God for specific purposes.

God's Preferred Communication Method

Throughout history, the almighty Creator has chosen not to physically descend from His celestial abode to converse with humans. While there are few instances in the Scriptures where God's voice was audibly heard on earth, primarily during Jesus' time, the general means through which God conveyed His messages was via angels. (Matthew 3:17; 17:5; John 12:28) Even the holy Law, bestowed upon the Israelites at Mount Sinai, was communicated through these celestial beings. Apostle Paul reinforces this by saying, "It was put in place through angels by an intermediary."—Galatians 3:19.

Encounters with God's Spokespersons

Acts 7:38 makes it evident that Moses was conversing with an angel when he was at Mount Sinai: "This is the one who was in the congregation in the wilderness with the angel who spoke to him at Mount Sinai." This angel acted on behalf of Jehovah, communicating as if God Himself was speaking.

Another significant account is when Moses encountered the burning thornbush. Here, "Jehovah's angel" appears to Moses and directly communicates with him, yet the words are as if they are from Jehovah Himself. When this angel spoke, it was as if God was communicating directly to Moses. (Exodus 3:2, 4, 6; Exodus 4:10)

The tale of Gideon, as captured in Judges 6, further illustrates this dynamic. Gideon interacted with a divine messenger referred to as "Jehovah's angel". Yet, as they converse, the narrative unfolds as though Gideon is speaking directly with Jehovah. Gideon acknowledges this unique experience when he remarks, "I have seen Jehovah's angel face to face!" This angel was delivering God's exact words, making Gideon's conversation with him synonymous with speaking directly to God.

In another instance, Samson's parents, Manoah and his wife, encountered a heavenly messenger. While they address and regard this angel as the direct representation of the divine, they acknowledge their indirect interaction with God through this envoy. Manoah's reaction encapsulates this sentiment when he exclaims, "We shall positively die, because it is God that we have seen," even though they were witnessing an angel, not Jehovah Himself. (Judges 13:2-18; Jg 13:22)

Drawing the Distinction

These accounts shed light on Abraham's interaction with the materialized angel, where the Scripture recounts "Jehovah appeared to him."—Genesis 18:1. Just like a telephone or radio conveys messages precisely, the angelic representatives of God transmitted His exact words. Thus, individuals like Abraham, Moses, and Manoah could engage with these celestial beings as though they were in direct conversation with Jehovah.

However, it is pivotal to understand the distinction: while these individuals might have witnessed these celestial beings and possibly experienced a reflection of God's magnificence through them, they never saw Jehovah God in His true form. This aligns perfectly with the apostle John's declaration: "No man has seen God at any time." (John 1:18) In essence, they were in the company of divine representatives, not the Creator Himself.

CHAPTER 7 Who Is Michael the Archangel?

Who is the Archangel?

"Archangel" is derived from the Greek term "archangelos." Among the spiritual beings referred to in the Bible, only Michael bears the title of "archangel." Some scholars have conjectured the possibility of other archangels existing, but the term's prefix, "arch," translates to "chief" or "principal," suggesting the uniqueness and singularity of the title. There's only one archangel: the principal angel. While the angel Gabriel is a powerful figure in Scripture, at no point is he addressed as an archangel. If there were a multitude of archangels, the term "arch" (meaning "chief" or "principal") would be misleading. Significantly, the term "archangel" always appears in the singular throughout the Scriptures, never in plural form. This emphasizes Michael's unique status as the sole archangel. Positioned as the highest-ranking angel, similar to the foremost general in a military hierarchy, Michael operates directly under God's command, leading other angels, including Gabriel, according to God's divine plan and purposes.

Michael's Name and Roles

Michael's name poses a rhetorical question: "Who is like God?" This archangel is prominently mentioned in several significant biblical events. He contended with Satan over Moses' body as detailed in Jude 9. Michael, along with Gabriel, vigilantly protected the Israelites, often confronting demonic forces that sought their harm (Daniel 10:13, 21). Michael played a pivotal role in banishing Satan and his demons from heaven (Revelation 12:7-9). He will also play a crucial role during the end times, vanquishing earthly rulers and their armies during Armageddon. Additionally, Michael will have the distinct honor of consigning Satan, God's primary adversary, to the abyss. – Revelation 18:1-2; 19:11-21.

The Defender of God's Sovereignty

Across the Scriptures, Michael's presence is consistently associated with intense, decisive actions. He is frequently depicted in confrontations with wicked angels in the Book of Daniel. The Epistle of Jude recounts his dispute with Satan. The Book of Revelation narrates his celestial battle against the Devil and his legion of demons. Michael, as the chief messenger, staunchly upholds God's sovereignty, epitomizing the essence of his name: "Who Is like God?"

Just as the supreme officer in an army remains undefeated regardless of the adversary's strength, Michael's might remains unparalleled. As described in Revelation, a monumental celestial battle ensues between Michael, leading God's faithful angels, and the dragon. Notably, Michael isn't a standalone entity but commands an entire legion of God's loyal angels, including Gabriel. Furthermore, Michael operates under the direct leadership of Jesus Christ. – Matthew 13:41; 16:27; 24:31; 2 Thessalonians 1:7; 1 Peter 3:22; Revelation 19:14-16.

Michael the Archangel Is Spoken of in the Following Texts.

Daniel 10:2, 13, 20-21 Updated American Standard Version (UASV)

[2] In those days I, Daniel, was mourning for three weeks. [13] The prince of the kingdom of Persia withstood me twenty-one days, but Michael, one of the chief princes, came to help me, for I was left there with the kings of Persia, [20] Then he said, "Do you know why I have come to you? But now I will return to fight against the prince of Persia; and when I go out, look, the prince of Greece will come. [21] But I will tell you what is inscribed in the book of truth, and there is none who contends by my side against these except Michael, your prince.

Introduction to the Archangel Michael

The book of Daniel, in its tenth chapter, sets the stage for the climactic vision that depicts the clashes between the Kings of the South and the North. Within these sacred pages, we encounter Michael, a chief figure in the celestial realm.

Rebel Angels and Their Limitations

After a cataclysmic event known as the flood, rebellious angels, who once had the power to take human forms, found themselves restrained. These celestial beings, once part of Jehovah God's faithful messengers, misused their capabilities, choosing to materialize in human form and engage in relationships with "the daughters of man" (Genesis 7:9-10). The Bible suggests that these deviant angels were stripped of their unique abilities after the flood, with their subsequent actions being limited to spirit possession.

Jude 1:6 sheds light on these fallen angels' fate. These angels, who defied their celestial boundaries, now find themselves shackled in "eternal chains under gloomy darkness." This isn't so much a physical place but a condition – a significant reduction in their powers, comparable to the constraints of a maximum-security prison.

Although these angels have lost their power to take human forms, they can still possess humans, save for God's true servants. Under Satan's guidance, they maintain control over the world's affairs. This influence over world events and nations stems from a structured hierarchy of demons, with Satan at the helm.

Daniel's Encounter and Revelation

Daniel's deep concern for his people post their Babylonian captivity led him to pray fervently for three weeks. God dispatched a benevolent angel to comfort Daniel. However, this angel was obstructed in his mission, explaining to Daniel that the "prince of the kingdom of Persia" hindered him for twenty-one days (Daniel 10:2, 13).

It's imperative to understand that this "prince" wasn't the earthly Persian King Cyrus, who was, in fact, favorable to Daniel and the Israelites. No mortal could possibly detain a mighty angel, especially when one recalls the might of an angel single-handedly defeating 185,000 Assyrian warriors overnight (Isaiah 37:36). Thus, this "prince of Persia" was none other than a malevolent celestial entity, a demon given dominion over the Persian Empire by Satan. Furthermore, the angel revealed that after this battle, he would contend with another demon, "the prince of Greece" (Daniel 10:20). This paints a picture of an organized hierarchy of demonic "princes" or rulers governing various territories under Satan's leadership.

John Walvoord, a renowned theologian, writes about Daniel 10:13, clarifying that this "prince" isn't the human Persian king but rather a demonic counterpart. Walvoord's viewpoint resonates with the consensus that demonic forces, to some degree, govern earthly kingdoms. Max Anders further elucidates that these demon "princes" exert influence over their assigned earthly territories, with Michael possibly serving as Israel's guardian angel.

Michael's Distinct Role

Michael's name and role hold immense significance in the heavenly realm. This chief angel stands as a stalwart defender of God's sovereignty, constantly battling against demonic forces. From opposing the "prince of Persia" to contending with other demonic entities, Michael's dedication to upholding God's rule remains unshaken. It's this very dedication and power that make Michael unique, placing him at the pinnacle of the angelic hierarchy. As the sole archangel, Michael oversees all of God's loyal messengers and safeguards His devout followers.

The Role of Michael in End Times

In the prophetic writings of Daniel, Michael is introduced as a figure of immense importance. As we observe in Daniel 12:1, during the final confrontation at Armageddon, Michael, the archangel, and notably the mightiest among all angels, will rise to defend the "sons of your people." This confrontation will lead to unprecedented distress, the "great tribulation". At this pivotal juncture, the salvation of those inscribed in the Book of Life is promised.

Michael's Historical Protection

Historically, Michael was perceived as the guardian angel of Israel, as highlighted by scholars such as Walvoord and Anders. However, this relationship took a turn as expressed in Jesus' words, denoting the shift of God's favor from Israel to the "Israel of God," i.e., Christianity (Matthew 21:45, 23:37-39; Galatians 6:15-16). This means that while Michael might have served as the protector for ancient Israel, his role now pivots towards defending true Christianity, the new "Israel of God." He isn't a guardian for individual Christians but leads a celestial army to defend them against malevolent forces.

Michael's Encounters with Satan

In Jude 1:9-10, a mysterious event is recounted. Here, Michael is depicted disputing with Satan over Moses' body. Instead of resorting to slander or abuse, Michael simply retorts with, "The Lord rebuke you!" This restrained response from such a powerful archangel emphasizes his unwavering respect for divine authority. Walls and Anders shed light on this event, suggesting that Michael was entrusted with Moses' burial following his death atop Mount Nebo. Jewish traditions, as supported by this passage, hint at Satan's claim to Moses' body, resulting in this celestial confrontation.

The Great War in Heaven

The apocalyptic literature in Revelation 12:7 unveils a cosmic conflict between Michael, leading God's loyal angels, and the dragon, with its demonic legions. This celestial "Star Wars-esque" clash symbolizes the eternal battle between good and evil, reflecting the sentiment of Ephesians 6:12 about our struggle not being against mortal beings, but against malevolent spiritual forces.

Although Christ is the supreme warrior of heaven, He makes His grand entrance only in Revelation 19. In contrast, Michael, the only archangel named in the Bible, holds a unique position as the commander of angels. This role is evident in Revelation and Jude 9. Some scholars like Easley may refer to Michael's role as a "bit part," but this archangel's significance cannot be understated. Michael has been at the forefront, guiding and protecting the chosen people, ever since humanity's initial fall in Eden.

In conclusion, Michael, the archangel, stands as a testament to God's unyielding power and His promise to protect the faithful against the forces of darkness.

Who Is the Angel of the Lord?

An Overview of Angelic References in Scripture

When we delve into the pages of the Bible, a notable figure that often surfaces is the "Angel of the Lord." Numerous references, from Genesis to Acts, indicate the significant appearances and interactions of this angelic entity with humans. Several scriptures such as Gen. 16:7, Ex. 3:2, Judges 6:11, 2 Sam. 24:16, and many others, attest to this being's prominent involvement in various biblical narratives.

Hierarchy Among the Angels

Among the heavenly hosts, Michael the archangel stands out as the pinnacle of angelic might and majesty. His frequent mention in the Scriptures, including in Daniel, Jude, and Revelation, underscores his unmatched rank and role among all heavenly beings. Michael is often referred to as "the great prince who stands guard over the sons of your people," suggesting his pivotal role in safeguarding God's chosen people and leading them, as inferred from passages like Exodus 23:20-23.

Other distinguished angels include the seraphs, as described in Isaiah 6:2, 6. The cherubs, mentioned around 90 times in Scripture, also hold a significant rank among angelic beings, as evident from their descriptions and the tasks assigned to them in passages like Genesis 3:24 and Ezekiel 10:1-22.

There is also a broader angelic body, which serves multifaceted roles. These angels act as communicators between God and humanity, guardians, protectors, executors of divine judgments, and bearers of salvation messages. Their actions span the range from shielding God's chosen to bringing forth God's wrath upon the wicked, as demonstrated in narratives like Genesis 19:1-26 and Matthew 24:29-31.

Addressing Misconceptions

It's essential to address some prevalent misconceptions about the "Angel of the Lord." Some, like William Smith in his "Bible Dictionary," contend that "the angel of the Lord" is a pre-incarnate manifestation of God or even Christ's visible form before his earthly incarnation. This perspective, however, isn't congruent with a careful reading of Scripture.

Another point of contention arises when Taylor associates the "Angel of the Lord" with Gabriel or even suggests an alignment with the Holy Spirit, as inferred from Acts 8:26, 29. This position isn't tenable. Gabriel, while undeniably a high-ranking angel with a close association with God, is distinct from the "Angel of the Lord." Moreover, equating this angel with the pre-incarnate Jesus doesn't hold water. The "Angel of the Lord," though powerful and authoritative, remains a creation and, therefore, subservient to Jesus.

In conclusion, while the "Angel of the Lord" has immense authority and is influential in the biblical narrative, it is essential to discern and differentiate this entity from God, Jesus Christ, and other significant angelic figures. Proper understanding aids in preventing theological inaccuracies and fosters a richer appreciation of the intricate tapestry of celestial beings depicted in Scripture.

CHAPTER 8 Who Is Gabriel?

Gabriel, whose name translates to the **"Able-Bodied One of God,"** holds the distinction of being one of the only two holy angels explicitly named in the Scriptures. Alongside Michael, Gabriel stands as a prominent figure in the biblical narrative, recognized not only for his significant role but also as the sole materialized angel to reveal his name to humans.

Gabriel's Appearances in the Book of Daniel

Gabriel's presence in the Bible is highlighted through his significant interactions with the prophet Daniel. His first notable appearance is by the Ulai River during "the third year of the kingship of Belshazzar." Here, Gabriel took on the pivotal role of interpreter, elucidating Daniel's vision of the he-goat and the ram. (Da 8:1, 15-26)

In another encounter, this time during "the first year of Darius" the Mede, Gabriel conveyed the crucial prophecy concerning the **"seventy weeks."** This prophecy stands as a foundational text in understanding certain timelines and events in biblical prophecy. (Da 9:1, 20-27)

Announcements of Births

Gabriel's role wasn't limited to communicating prophecies. He was also entrusted with heralding the births of pivotal figures in biblical history. An instance of this is when he appeared to Zechariah the priest. Gabriel joyfully announced that Zechariah and his elderly wife, Elizabeth, would be blessed with a son, who would later be known as John the Baptizer. This was no ordinary proclamation, as John was foreordained to play a significant role as the forerunner of Jesus Christ. (Lu 1:11-20)

In another paramount revelation, Gabriel visited Mary, a young virgin betrothed to Joseph. In his greeting, he acclaimed, **"Greetings, O favored one, the Lord is with you!"** He then unveiled to Mary the miraculous news that she would conceive and give birth to a son, Jesus. This son, Gabriel declared, would be designated as the **"Son of the Most High."** He would inherit "the throne of David his father" and would establish a kingdom that would have no end. This monumental message highlighted Jesus' unparalleled role in God's purpose. (Lu 1:26-38)

Characteristics and Position of Gabriel

Drawing from the Scriptural accounts, we discern that Gabriel occupies a prominent position among the heavenly hosts. He is depicted as a top-tier angel, one closely associated with the divine court, and is described as one **"who stands near before God."** Such a title underscores his intimate proximity and association with the Almighty. He is dispatched by God Himself, "sent forth" to deliver God's special messages to His servants on earth. (Lu 1:19, 26) When appearing to humans, Gabriel's form, be it in a vision or materialized, embodies the essence of his name, projecting the image of an **"a man."** (Da 8:15) "And it came about when I, Daniel, had seen the vision, I sought to understand it. And look, there stood before me one having the appearance of **a man**"

Gabriel's roles and interactions in the Bible paint a portrait of an angel deeply involved in the execution of God's purpose. As a messenger, interpreter, and herald, Gabriel's contributions are immeasurable, emphasizing his esteemed position in the heavenly realms and his unwavering service to Jehovah God.

CHAPTER 9 Rebellion in the Spirit Realm

The Abundance of Spirit Beings

The Bible offers a profound insight into the existence of a multitude of spirit beings. Central to this is the truth that Jehovah, being a spirit, was the original entity in the universe. (John 4:24; 2 Corinthians 3:17, 18)

Before our planet came into existence, Jehovah embarked on a grand work: the creation of a vast assembly of spirit beings, or angels. Endowed with greater power and intellect than humans, these angels were numerous beyond comprehension. In fact, a vision granted to Daniel revealed the staggering sight of a hundred million angels! (Daniel 7:10; Hebrews 1:7) It's essential to understand that these spirit beings predated the earth and were not spirits of deceased humans. In simple terms, Jehovah's creation comprised millions upon millions of spirit entities.

The Onset of Rebellion in the Heavenly Realm

Despite the harmonious beginning, dissension arose in the spirit realm. Initially, every angelic being was upright and faithful. However, a single angel deviated from the righteous path, earning the infamous title: Satan the Devil. Consumed by ambition, Satan coveted the worship directed toward Jehovah by the earthly inhabitants. His sinister plot unfolded as follows:

In Eden's idyllic setting, a plethora of trees bore delectable fruits. Jehovah granted Adam and Eve the freedom to relish these fruits, with one notable exception: the tree of the knowledge of good and evil.

Jehovah explicitly warned them that consumption of its fruit would result in death. (Genesis 2:9, 16, 17)

In a devious ploy, Satan manipulated a serpent to converse with Eve, falsely promising her God-like wisdom and immortality if she consumed the forbidden fruit. Tragically, Eve succumbed to this deception, consuming the fruit and later sharing it with Adam. (Genesis 3:1-6)

This historical account uncovers Satan's nature as a treacherous liar. Contrary to his assurance, Eve and Adam indeed faced death due to their disobedience. While Satan remains alive for now, his eventual fate is sealed: his sins will lead to his destruction. Nevertheless, in his limited time, he relentlessly seeks to deceive humanity and lure them away from God's righteous path. (John 8:44)

Further Angelic Defection

Satan's rebellion was only the beginning. As time progressed, additional angels became corrupted. These angels, captivated by the allure of earthly women, descended to the human realm, assuming male forms to indulge in forbidden relationships. This was a gross violation of God's intended order. (Genesis 6:1, 2; Jude 6)

Their union with human women produced offspring that were far from ordinary: violent giants who spread chaos across the earth. Their wickedness reached such unprecedented levels that Jehovah deemed it necessary to cleanse the earth with a cataclysmic flood, sparing only the righteous Noah and his family. (Genesis 6:4, 11; 7:23)

While the deluge eradicated the wicked from the earth, the fallen angels retreated to the spirit realm. Though they escaped immediate death, they faced severe consequences. Jehovah cast them out of His holy congregation of angels, stripping them of their privilege to assume human forms. Their fate is grim, as they will eventually face destruction in God's final judgment. (2 Peter 2:4; Jude 6)

Satan Cast Out of Heaven

Understanding the "Last Days"

When Paul wrote to Timothy in 2 Timothy 3:1, his words carried a sense of urgency and gravity: "But realize this, that in the last days difficult times will come." The term "last days" doesn't refer to a distant event in the future. Instead, it signifies the current epoch, initiated by Jesus Christ himself. This era will span uninterrupted until Christ's return, and while it is marked by the magnificent grace of God, bringing forth salvation and the establishment of the church, it is simultaneously fraught with danger. The "last days" are characterized by Satan's relentless onslaughts, as he seeks to thwart and subvert God's grand redemptive plans.

Paul's intent in providing this information was clear. He wished for believers to be vigilant and spiritually fortified, knowing well that the battle with evil would intensify. Every believer is faced with a choice: to actively prepare for the impending challenges or to choose the path of personal comfort and safety.

The Celestial War in the First Century

Revelation, one of the books in the Bible, provides an intricate depiction of a monumental conflict that took place in heaven during the first century CE:

"7 And war broke out in heaven: Michael [the archangel] and his angels made war with the dragon, and the dragon and its angels waged war, 8 but they were not strong enough, nor was a place found for them any longer in heaven. 9 And the great dragon was thrown down, the serpent of old who is called the devil and Satan, who deceives the whole inhabited earth; he was thrown down to the earth, and his angels were thrown down with him."

This celestial skirmish had profound consequences:

"Therefore, rejoice, O heavens and you who dwell in them!" The heavens could celebrate the expulsion of Satan and his malevolent angels. However, the situation on earth was more dire: "Woe to you, O earth and sea, for the devil has come down to you in great wrath, because he knows he has a short time." —Revelation 12:7-9, 12.

This alarming reality underscores the peril posed by Satan and his malevolent cohorts on humanity. These rebellious angels, known as demons, are God's adversaries. Their singular intent is to sow discord, chaos, and misery. Every single one of them embodies malevolence and evil.

Historical Atrocities Attributed to Demons

Satan and his demonic followers have been historically recognized for their malevolence and their penchant for causing harm. Their actions, driven by cruelty and spite, have resulted in great suffering for many. One of the earliest accounts of their destructive behavior can be found in the story of Job, a faithful servant of God.

In the narrative, Satan unleashed his wrath on Job's life in staggering ways. Initially, he decimated Job's livestock and brutally murdered his servants. But his malevolence didn't stop there. In a tragic turn of events, Satan caused "a great wind" to collapse the house where Job's ten children were, resulting in their deaths. Later, Satan tormented Job physically, afflicting him with "loathsome skin sores from the sole of his foot up to the crown of his head." The aim was clear: to break Job's spirit and challenge his unwavering faith in God.—Job 1:7-19; 2:7.

Demonic Acts During Jesus' Era

The New Testament further reveals the menacing actions of demons. In Jesus' time, these sinister beings continued their campaign of chaos and torment against humanity. Various accounts show them possessing and harming individuals in cruel ways.

In certain instances, the demons rendered individuals mute and blind, effectively robbing them of their senses and abilities to communicate. —Matthew 9:32, 33; 12:22. Another disturbing account from the Book of Mark describes a man under demonic possession, compelled to self-harm by slashing himself with stones. —Mark 5:5. Perhaps one of the most harrowing accounts is found in the Book of Luke, where a young boy is described as being tormented by a demon that provoked him to scream, violently convulse, and thrash himself onto the ground. —Luke 9:42.

Such accounts vividly illustrate the destructive intentions of demons and the sheer magnitude of pain and suffering they inflict upon their victims.

CHAPTER 10 The Devil's Influence on Humanity: Can He Control You?

Understanding the Devil's Reach

The Bible provides insight into the profound influence the Devil and demons exert on humanity. It goes as far as to state, "The Evil One controls the whole world." (1 John 5:19, New Century Version). To understand the extent of the Devil's influence, it's essential to explore the various means through which he operates.

Methods of Devil's Influence

1. **Deception:** Christians are advised to be on guard and to "fight against the devil's evil tricks." (Ephesians 6:11, NCV). Deception is a primary tool in the Devil's arsenal. He can manipulate individuals into mistaking his agents as true servants of God, thus leading them astray.—2 Corinthians 11:13-15.

2. **Spiritism:** The Devil employs various forms of spiritism to deceive. This includes using spirit mediums, fortune-tellers, and those engaging in divination or astrology. Activities like drug use, hypnotism, and certain meditation techniques that promote an empty mind can also make individuals susceptible to demonic influences.—Luke 11:24-26.

3. **False Religion:** Religions promoting false doctrines divert people from following the true path of God. (1 Corinthians 10:20) Such misleading doctrines are referred to as "teachings of demons" in the scriptures.—1 Timothy 4:1.

4. **Possession:** There are biblical accounts of demons taking over individuals, influencing their actions and behaviors. Such possession sometimes resulted in physical ailments or self-harm. Examples include being rendered blind, mute, or even inflicting injuries upon oneself.—Matthew 12:22; Mark 5:2-5.

Shielding Yourself from the Devil's Influence

Though the Devil's influence is pervasive, one need not succumb to fear or anxiety regarding demonic control. The Bible offers guidance on how to resist and counteract such influences:

- **Awareness:** It's vital to be aware of the Devil's strategies to ensure you are "not ignorant of his designs."—2 Corinthians 2:11.

- **Biblical Knowledge and Application:** Immersing oneself in the teachings of the Bible and putting into practice its principles acts as a shield against the Devil's ploys. This knowledge acts as an armor, providing protection against any spiritual onslaught.—Ephesians 6:11-18.

- **Purge Demonic Associations:** Any items or influences associated with demonic activities should be eliminated from one's life. This extends to music, books, magazines, and other media that promote or glamorize spiritism. (Acts 19:19)

In essence, while the Devil possesses significant influence over the world, individuals have the tools and knowledge, as provided by the scriptures, to resist and combat his deceptive tactics.

CHAPTER 11 Can Satan Read Our Thoughts?

Satan's Limitations

There's a question that many ponder: Can Satan, also known as the Devil, tap into our innermost thoughts? Delving into biblical scriptures, the evidence suggests that neither Satan nor his cohorts of demons possess the capability to penetrate the depths of our minds.

Descriptive Titles and Their Implications

Examining Satan's titles in the scriptures provides insight. He's designated as the Resister (Satan), the Slanderer (Devil), the Deceiver (Serpent), the Tempter, and the Liar. (Job 1:6; Matthew 4:3; John 8:44; 2 Corinthians 11:3; Revelation 12:9). Notably, none of these titles suggest an innate ability to delve into human thoughts.

God's Exclusive Ability

In sharp contrast, Jehovah God uniquely possesses this profound capability. He's depicted as the one who "tests [or inspects] hearts." (Proverbs 17:3; 1 Samuel 16:7; 1 Chronicles 29:17) Furthermore, Hebrews 4:13 proclaims: "no creature is hidden from his [God's] sight, but all are naked and exposed to the eyes of him to whom we must give account." Significantly, this profound power extends to Jesus Christ, God's Son. Jesus affirmed: "I am he who searches mind and heart, and I will give to each of you according to your works."—Revelation 2:23.

It's vital to highlight that the scriptures never attribute such a heart and mind searching ability to Satan. Considering the Bible's extensive insights into Satan's methods, this omission is significant.

Satan's Observational Abilities

Yet, this doesn't negate Satan's astute observational skills. He's had millennia to observe, analyze, and comprehend human behaviors, emotions, and vulnerabilities. He doesn't need telepathic abilities when he can interpret our actions, our entertainment choices, our conversations, and even subtle cues like facial expressions and body language.

Satan's Modus Operandi

By and large, Satan reverts to his age-old strategies, reminiscent of those he employed in the garden of Eden: lies, deception, and misinformation. (Genesis 3:1-5) His goal is to corrupt, aiming to make Christians "depraved in mind and deprived of the truth." (1 Timothy 6:5) His world has unleashed a torrent of misleading information and entertainment. To counteract this, Christians must guard their minds by donning "the helmet of salvation" (Ephesians 6:17), immersing themselves in biblical truths and steering clear from Satan's world's distasteful elements.

The Christian's Defense

While Satan undeniably poses a threat, an overwhelming fear of him and his demons isn't warranted. Following the guidance in James 4:7: "Resist the devil, and he will flee from you," ensures one remains shielded. By adhering to this counsel, just as Jesus stated, Satan will find no foothold within us.—John 14:30.

Edward D. Andrews

CHAPTER 12 Our Struggle against Dark Spiritual Forces

The Prevalence of Wicked Spirits in Our World

The presence and influence of wicked spirits are undeniable when we study the Scriptures. From the fall in the Garden of Eden to various accounts in the New Testament, these spiritual entities consistently attempt to sway and deceive humanity. Their activity isn't merely confined to biblical times; it extends to our contemporary era, affecting our thoughts, actions, and societies.

Why the Activity of Wicked Spirits is of Particular Interest

Scriptural Warnings: Throughout the Scriptures, there are countless warnings about the deceptions and machinations of wicked spirits. Paul's letter to the Ephesians, for instance, warns us that "we do not wrestle against flesh and blood, but against the rulers, against the authorities, against the cosmic powers over this present darkness, against the spiritual forces of evil in the heavenly places" (Ephesians 6:12, UASV). This clear warning underscores the fact that our real battle is not against tangible human entities but against invisible spiritual forces.

Modern Manifestations: In our modern world, the manifestations of wicked spirits are evident in various forms. From ideologies that go against God's standards to societal norms that normalize sin, the influence of these spirits is palpable.

Personal Spiritual Health: Understanding and acknowledging the activity of these spirits is crucial for our spiritual health. Being ignorant of their devices can lead us into spiritual pitfalls. Peter admonishes us to "Be sober-minded; be watchful. Your adversary the devil prowls around like a roaring lion, seeking someone to devour" (1 Peter 5:8, UASV).

How to Triumph Over Wicked Spirit Forces

Given the profound influence and capabilities of these wicked spirits, one may wonder: How can mere mortals hope to withstand such powerful entities? Thankfully, the Scriptures provide a roadmap for victory.

Put on the Full Armor of God: In Ephesians 6:13-18, Paul uses the metaphor of a soldier's armor to describe the spiritual tools at our disposal. Each component, from the belt of truth to the sword of the Spirit, equips us to stand firm against the wicked one's assaults. By immersing ourselves in truth, living righteously, preaching the gospel, maintaining our faith, understanding salvation, and clinging to God's word, we can effectively shield ourselves.

Prayer and Vigilance: Regular communication with Jehovah is vital. Prayer serves as our lifeline, providing strength, wisdom, and guidance in our spiritual warfare. Coupled with vigilance, which entails being alert to spiritual threats, prayer fortifies us against demonic influences.

Fellowship and Community: The Christian community plays a pivotal role in our defense against wicked spirits. Hebrews 10:24-25 (UASV) stresses the importance of not forsaking the assembly and spurring one another to love and good deeds. Together, we can encourage, uplift, and warn each other, making us collectively stronger against spiritual adversaries.

Avoid Occult Practices: One direct way wicked spirits gain influence over individuals is through occult practices. The Scriptures expressly prohibit any involvement in spiritism, divination, or any form of sorcery (Deuteronomy 18:10-12). Engaging in these practices opens the door to demonic influence, making it paramount for Christians to steer clear.

Stay Rooted in the Scriptures: Consistent study and meditation on God's word provide knowledge and discernment. The Scriptures act as a spiritual filter, enabling us to distinguish truth from error. Psalm 119:105 (UASV) aptly describes God's word as "a lamp to my feet and a light to my path." By staying rooted in the Scriptures, we arm ourselves with the divine wisdom to detect and repel spiritual deceptions.

Repentance and Humility: Recognizing that we are prone to sin and imperfection, regular self-examination and repentance are necessary. When we err, approaching Jehovah with a contrite heart and seeking forgiveness shields us from the further influence of wicked spirits. Proverbs 28:13 (UASV) "He who conceals his transgressions will not prosper, but he who confesses and forsakes them will obtain mercy." This Scripture emphasizes the protective power of humility and repentance in our spiritual warfare. Recognizing our weaknesses and turning to Jehovah for strength and forgiveness blocks the avenues through which wicked spirits can gain a foothold.

The Power of Christ's Sacrifice: Understanding and appreciating the significance of Jesus Christ's ransom sacrifice grants us another layer of protection. Christ's death and resurrection not only opened the way for salvation but also delivered a decisive blow to Satan and his forces. Colossians 2:15 (UASV) says, "[God] disarmed the rulers and authorities and put them to open shame, by triumphing over them in [Christ]." By exercising faith in this sacrifice, we align ourselves with the ultimate victor in the cosmic struggle against wicked spirits.

Maintain a Strong Spiritual Routine: Just as physical immunity gets bolstered by a consistent regimen of healthy habits, our spiritual immunity gets fortified by regular spiritual routines. This includes consistent Bible study, regular prayer, participation in Christian meetings, and engaging in the ministry. Such habits nourish our spirit and build a robust defense against spiritual threats.

Seeking Heavenly Assistance: Remember that while we wrestle against wicked spirits, we are not alone in this fight. Jehovah dispatches his loyal angels to guard and guide his faithful servants. Psalms 91:11 (UASV) assures us, "For he will command his angels concerning you to guard you in all your ways." By praying for and seeking heavenly intervention, we enlist powerful allies in our struggle against demonic forces.

The Battle is Winnable

The struggle against wicked spirits might seem daunting given their superhuman power and millennia of experience. However, Jehovah has not left us defenseless. He has provided an array of tools, guidance, and assistance to ensure that we can stand firm against spiritual adversaries. By leaning on Jehovah, understanding our enemy, and employing the spiritual resources at our disposal, victory in this crucial battle is not just possible; it's assured. As Romans 8:37 (UASV) proclaims, "In all these things we are more than conquerors through him who loved us." In the end, with Jehovah on our side, the wicked spirits stand no chance.

Wrestling Against Wicked Spirit Forces

The spiritual warfare that true Christians face is intense, especially in these critical times we live in. An understanding of whom our true enemies are, the methods they employ, and the powerful backing we have can fortify us in our fight against these unseen yet very real adversaries.

Whom Does Satan Viciously Oppose, and How?

Satan's Primary Target: Satan's primary adversary and target is Jehovah God. Since he cannot harm Jehovah directly, he turns his attention to Jehovah's loyal servants and creation. In the garden of Eden, his deceptive tactics led to the sin of Adam and Eve, effectively severing their perfect relationship with God. As history progressed, Satan has constantly been at work, trying to destroy the faith and loyalty of God's servants.

Satan's Focus on Jesus: The most profound demonstration of Satan's opposition was towards Jesus Christ. From trying to have him killed shortly after birth using King Herod (Matthew 2:13-18) to the temptations in the wilderness (Matthew 4:1-11), Satan's objective was clear: prevent Jesus from accomplishing his earthly mission. However, despite these vicious attacks, Jesus remained faithful, setting a sterling example for his followers.

Satan's Attack on Modern-Day Christians: Now, Satan has shifted his focus on those who follow Jesus' footsteps. He disseminates false doctrines, promotes divisive ideologies, and tempts Christians into immoral conduct, seeking to divert them from the path of righteousness.

The Source of the Power of Human Governments and its Authentication

Earthly Rulers and Their Power: The Bible indicates that all authority on earth originates from Jehovah. Romans 13:1 (UASV) states, "Let every person be in subjection to the governing authorities. For there is no authority except from God, and those which exist are established by God." However, this doesn't mean every action of these governments is divinely approved.

Satan's Dominion Over Earthly Governments: Despite the initial source of power being God, Satan has significant control over the world's political systems. This control is evident when he tempted Jesus, offering him "all the kingdoms of the world" if Jesus worshipped him (Matthew 4:8-9). Jesus did not dispute Satan's claim to these kingdoms, highlighting the Devil's dominion over them.

Gathering of Political Rulers in Our Time

Significance of Revelation's Prophecy: The book of Revelation foretells a gathering of "kings of the entire inhabited earth" for "the war of the great day of God the Almighty" (Revelation 16:14, UASV). This global unification of governments, to some extent, can be observed in international collaborations and alliances.

Satan's Role in this Unification: As Satan knows his time is limited (Revelation 12:12), he is desperate. He works behind the scenes, influencing political systems to oppose God's will and purposes, bringing them together in opposition to God's Kingdom.

Avoiding Unwitting Support to the Satanic System

The Allure of the World's System: Satan's world can be alluring, with its promises of wealth, power, and pleasure. But as Christians, we are urged to be no part of it (John 17:16). We must recognize the temporary nature of such enticements and the spiritual danger they pose.

Steer Clear of Divisive Issues: Topics like politics can be divisive. While Christians respect governmental authority, they refrain from being deeply embroiled in political affairs, realizing that true and lasting change comes only through God's Kingdom.

Regular Spiritual Nourishment: Consistently feeding on God's word, the Bible, helps us discern right from wrong and strengthens our resolve to remain neutral in worldly affairs. Regular prayer and association with fellow believers can also fortify our determination.

Navigating through life in Satan's world requires more than physical strength or intellectual prowess; it demands spiritual vigilance. Satan, described as "the god of this system of things," is not only powerful but also cunning. (2 Corinthians 4:4, UASV) His deceptive methods, designed to lead astray even the most dedicated servants of Jehovah, must be discerned and resisted. This article aims to expose some of Satan's most subtle tactics.

Satan's Use of False Religion

The Grand Deception: One of Satan's masterstrokes has been his use of false religion. He has created a labyrinth of religious beliefs, each claiming to be the path to God, causing confusion and leading many astray. By doing so, he obscures the genuine path to God and His true teachings.

Blurring the Lines: Even for those dedicated to Jehovah, the danger exists. Satan blends elements of truth with falsehoods in religions, making them appear as light. This amalgamation can draw believers into practices that are not genuinely Scriptural. For example, traditions that have pagan origins might be integrated into religious ceremonies under the guise of Christian worship.

The Subtle Lure of Immorality

Satan's Exploitation of Sex: Sex, a beautiful gift from Jehovah intended to bond married couples and for procreation, has been twisted by Satan. The world today is inundated with sexual imagery, promoting casual and illicit sexual conduct. These depictions desensitize individuals, making immoral acts seem normal and acceptable.

Changing Attitudes Towards Immorality and Violence: Through media, literature, and popular culture, Satan has normalized violence and immorality. What was once considered shocking becomes commonplace, subtly altering our moral compass. This shift can lead believers to rationalize or justify behaviors and attitudes that are contrary to Scriptural standards.

The Traps of Spiritism

The Deceptive Allure: Even those knowledgeable about the dangers of spiritism can be ensnared if they aren't vigilant. How? Spiritism isn't always overt. It can be hidden in popular entertainment, in books, movies, or television shows that glamorize the supernatural.

Subtle Introductions: Elements of spiritism might be introduced as mere fiction or harmless fun. However, by consuming such content, we expose ourselves to ideas and practices that Jehovah condemns.

Engaging, even passively, can open the door to further exploration and eventual acceptance.

Music's Powerful Influence

Sonic Manipulations: Music, in itself a beautiful form of expression, can be harnessed by Satan to promote ungodly thoughts and behaviors. Certain genres or songs glorify violence, immorality, or rebellion against God. The catchy melodies can implant these ideas in our minds, leading us to meditate on things that displease Jehovah.

Fashion, Appearance, and Speech: Silent Indicators of Admiration

Imitating the World's Standards: Admiration for worldly lifestyles can manifest in our clothing, hairstyle, or manner of speech. Adopting styles or behaviors popularized by celebrities or individuals who promote ungodly lifestyles can indicate a subtle alignment with their values.

More Than Just Appearance: It's not about being old-fashioned or out-of-touch. It's about recognizing that our outward appearance and speech reflect our inner values. Aligning with those whose lifestyles God disapproves of can slowly erode our spiritual standards.

Safeguarding Ourselves Against Satan's Schemes

Constant Vigilance: Recognizing Satan's strategies is crucial. However, awareness alone isn't sufficient; proactive measures are essential. This involves regular Bible study, which acts as a protective barrier, fortifying our minds against harmful influences. By immersing ourselves in Jehovah's words and principles, we're equipped with the necessary tools to discern right from wrong.

Prayer – Our Spiritual Lifeline: Engaging in earnest prayer is like having a direct line to Jehovah. Seeking His guidance, expressing our anxieties, and asking for strength to resist temptations are vital. James 4:7-8 (UASV) reminds us to "submit yourselves therefore to God. Resist the devil, and he will flee from you. Draw near to God, and he will draw near to you." Prayer is a means by which we draw close to our Heavenly Father, and in doing so, we gain the strength to fend off Satan's advances.

Healthy Association: Surrounding ourselves with fellow believers who are also striving to maintain high moral standards creates a support system. Together, we can encourage one another, share experiences, and provide counsel based on the Scriptures. This unity in purpose and mutual encouragement acts as a bulwark against Satan's attempts to divide and conquer.

Action Based on Knowledge: It's not enough to know what's right; we must act on that knowledge. This might mean making changes in our lifestyle, eliminating certain forms of entertainment, or even distancing ourselves from associations that pull us away from Jehovah. Every decision should be weighed against the question: 'Does this draw me closer to Jehovah or push me away?'

Staying Active in Christian Activities: Engaging in Christian meetings, field service, and other congregation activities reinforces our spiritual routine. These activities not only provide spiritual nourishment but also create opportunities for us to fortify others, making the entire congregation stronger against Satan's attacks.

In conclusion, the battle against Satan's cunning devices is relentless, but it's not one we fight alone. Jehovah has provided us with a comprehensive arsenal: His Word, prayer, the Christian congregation, and His holy spirit. By making full use of these provisions and staying alert, we can confidently navigate through Satan's world, not as helpless victims but as triumphant warriors, always ready to "stand firm against the schemes of the Devil." (Ephesians 6:11, UASV)

Conquering Satan's World Despite Our Imperfections

When considering the sheer might and cunning of Satan, it may seem daunting, if not impossible, for imperfect humans to resist his influence. After all, 1 John 5:19 (UASV) candidly states that "the whole world lies in the power of the evil one." However, Scripture assures us that with Jehovah's provisions, we can not only defend ourselves but also effectively conquer the spiritual challenges posed by Satan's world.

Our Imperfections vs. Jehovah's Strength: It's essential to recognize that while we are inherently imperfect due to inherited sin, Jehovah's power is limitless. Our imperfections do not make us weak when we lean on Jehovah's strength. The Apostle Paul, well aware of his imperfections, stated in Philippians 4:13 (UASV), "I can do all things through him who strengthens me." Thus, our victory over Satan's world is not by our might but by relying on Jehovah.

Understanding the Spiritual Armor: Ephesians 6:13-17

The Apostle Paul uses the analogy of a soldier's armor to describe the spiritual tools and defenses Jehovah provides. Let's delve into the benefits of each part of this spiritual armor.

The Belt of Truth: Truth stabilizes our spiritual stance. Just as a belt holds other pieces of a soldier's equipment in place, the truth about Jehovah and His purposes keeps our spiritual lives in order. In an age of misinformation and deceit, holding tight to the truth of the Scriptures is essential.

Breastplate of Righteousness: The breastplate protects vital organs, especially the heart. Righteousness, or living a life that aligns with Jehovah's standards, protects our figurative heart, our inner self, or motivations. By upholding Jehovah's righteous standards, we shield our hearts from corrupt influences and intentions.

Footwear of the Gospel: The imagery here is of a soldier's sandals, designed for long marches and tough terrains. Spreading the good news of the Kingdom is our mission, and being prepared with the "readiness" means we are always eager and willing to share the gospel, regardless of the challenges.

Shield of Faith: Faith, our deep trust in Jehovah, acts as a protective shield. Satan often throws "fiery darts" - doubts, fears, and lies. A robust and well-developed faith can extinguish these attacks, preventing them from shaking our resolve.

Helmet of Salvation: The helmet, vital for protecting the head in battle, represents our hope in salvation. By keeping our minds focused on the hope Jehovah provides, we guard ourselves against despair and stay motivated in our worship and service.

Sword of the Spirit: The only offensive weapon in the list, the "sword of the Spirit," is the Word of God. The Scriptures are our primary tool for teaching, correcting, and setting matters straight. It's also our primary means of defense against spiritual deception.

Taking the Offensive in Spiritual Warfare

While the armor provides defensive protection, Jehovah's servants are not merely to be passive. Here's how we can take the offensive:

Regular Bible Study: Delving deep into the Scriptures not only strengthens our faith but equips us to refute false teachings and provide answers to those genuinely seeking the truth.

Engaging in Prayer: James 5:16 (UASV) reminds us, "The prayer of a righteous person has great power as it is working." Regular communication with Jehovah is not just a means of seeking help but actively involves Him in our battles.

Evangelism: By actively spreading the good news of the Kingdom, we counteract the lies and negative influence of Satan's world. Each time we help a person come to the truth, it's a victory against the false narratives of the enemy.

Fellowship with Fellow Believers: Hebrews 10:24-25 (UASV) encourages us "not to forsake our assembling together, as is the custom of some, but encouraging one another." Being part of a community of believers provides mutual encouragement, strength, and support. In a world dominated by isolation and individualism, united worship and fellowship act as a strong countermeasure. Sharing experiences, scriptural insights, and simply being there for one another fortify us against Satan's efforts to dishearten or mislead us.

Resisting Temptations and Testing: When faced with moral dilemmas or enticements to sin, actively resisting and seeking Jehovah's guidance is an offensive move against Satan's designs. 1 Corinthians 10:13 (UASV) assures us that Jehovah "will also provide the way of escape, that you may be able to endure it." Our proactive effort in seeking that way of escape and choosing it is our active stand against the enemy.

Promoting Godly Values: In a society often skewed against godly standards, championing virtues such as honesty, loyalty, self-sacrifice, and unconditional love is an act of defiance against the prevailing tide. By both living and advocating for these values, we showcase the superiority of Jehovah's standards over Satan's.

Engaging in Spiritual Self-Reflection: Periodically examining our spiritual health, motivations, and actions allows us to identify and address any weak spots or vulnerabilities. This proactive introspection keeps us spiritually agile and prepared for any of Satan's ploys.

In conclusion, while the challenge of facing a formidable adversary like Satan may seem daunting, Jehovah has not left us defenseless. He provides the tools, the armor, and the guidance necessary to not just defend ourselves but also to gain victories against wicked spirit forces. The Apostle Paul sums up our situation and the assurance we have in Romans 8:37 (UASV), "But in all these things we overwhelmingly conquer through him who loved us." With Jehovah on our side, and by using the provisions he has given, we can and will be more than conquerors.

CHAPTER 13 The Importance of Learning About Angels

The unseen realm of spirit creatures plays a significant role in the Scriptures and in our lives as followers of Jehovah. Understanding the nature, role, and activities of these creatures is pivotal for several reasons.

Firstly, angels have been a part of Jehovah's purpose since before the foundation of the earth. Their interactions with humanity, both positive and negative, have shaped history and the course of human events. *A deeper knowledge of these beings will enrich our understanding of the Bible narrative and God's grand purpose.*

Secondly, the angels take a keen interest in humanity. The Apostle Peter tells us that "into these things angels long to look." (1 Peter 1:12, UASV) Their vested interest in the outworking of Jehovah's purpose and the salvation of humanity underscores their importance in the grand tapestry of creation.

Lastly, understanding the nature and activity of righteous angels can be a source of comfort. The Bible often portrays angels as Jehovah's messengers and instruments of protection for His servants. Being aware of their protective role can bolster our faith, especially in challenging times.

Origin of the Angels

Angels are spirit creatures created by Jehovah. They existed long before the physical universe and humanity came into being. Their existence is not a product of evolution or random chance, but a direct act of creation by Jehovah God.

Job 38:4-7 - A Glimpse into the Past

Job 38:4-7 (UASV) provides a fascinating insight into the time of the earth's foundation. Jehovah, in his discourse with Job, asks, "Where were you when I laid the foundation of the earth? ... when the morning stars sang together and all the sons of God shouted for joy?" This passage reveals a profound truth.

The term "morning stars" and "sons of God" are poetic descriptions of angels. This indicates that the angelic host was already in existence and rejoicing when Jehovah embarked on the project of terrestrial creation. They witnessed the raw display of Jehovah's creative power, shaping the earth and setting it in its place.

The angels' joyous reaction to creation underscores their closeness to Jehovah and their appreciation of His magnificent works. It also demonstrates their supportive role, not as mere passive observers but as active participants in praising and glorifying Jehovah. *Their jubilation serves as an affirmation of the righteousness and goodness of Jehovah's creative acts.*

The Vast Multitude of Angels

The Bible doesn't provide an exact number for the angels Jehovah created, but it does give us glimpses that suggest a vast multitude. Daniel 7:10, for instance, speaks of "thousands upon thousands" serving Him and "myriads upon myriads" standing before Him. This language emphasizes an innumerable host, a testament to Jehovah's grandeur and majesty.

Moreover, angels are not all identical; they have ranks, roles, and responsibilities. The Bible speaks of cherubs guarding the way to the tree of life in Genesis 3:24, seraphs surrounding Jehovah's throne in Isaiah 6, and archangels like Michael playing significant roles in events related to God's people (Daniel 12:1; Jude 9). This structured hierarchy and diversity showcase the wisdom of Jehovah in creating a well-ordered society of spirit creatures.

Our exploration into the realm of spirit creatures, particularly angels, is not a mere academic exercise. It enriches our appreciation of

Jehovah's grand design, strengthens our faith, and underscores Jehovah's loving provision of protection and guidance for His servants. Angels, as an integral part of Jehovah's purpose, play roles that intertwine with our lives and the outworking of Jehovah's will. As we continue to delve deeper into the Scriptures, our understanding and appreciation of these magnificent creatures will only grow, drawing us closer to our magnificent Creator, Jehovah.

The Deep Interest of Faithful Angels in Human Activities

The Scriptures leave no doubt that the faithful angels possess a profound interest in human activities. Jesus highlighted this fact when he said that "there is joy in the presence of the angels of God over one sinner who repents." (Luke 15:10, UASV) The implication here is clear: angels are not mere distant observers but are deeply involved emotionally and take delight in the spiritual progress of humans. *Their joy in witnessing repentance underscores the value of every individual in the eyes of Jehovah and his celestial servants.*

Biblical Examples of Angelic Support

Throughout the Scriptures, numerous examples provide compelling evidence of angelic intervention and support in the lives of Jehovah's servants:

1. **Protection of Lot**: In Genesis 19, two angels took on human form to lead Lot and his family out of Sodom, saving them from the impending divine judgment.

2. **Comforting Hagar**: An angel comforted Hagar in her distress, ensuring her and her son's safety. (Genesis 21:17-19)

3. **Daniel in the Lion's Den**: An angel shut the mouths of lions, protecting Daniel when he was thrown into a den for his unwavering faith. (Daniel 6:22)

4. **Peter's Jailbreak**: An angel miraculously delivered the Apostle Peter from prison, enabling him to continue his ministry. (Acts 12:7-10)

These accounts, among many others, highlight the active role of angels in supporting, protecting, and guiding Jehovah's servants. Their intervention showcases Jehovah's care for His people, employing His powerful spirit beings to execute His will and ensure the fulfillment of His purposes.

Angelic Protection in Our Times

Even though we live in an age where angels no longer appear visibly to God's people, their protective role hasn't diminished. As mentioned earlier, Psalm 34:7 provides the comforting assurance: "The angel of Jehovah encamps around those who fear him and delivers them." This Scripture affirms that God's powerful angels still shield His people, especially against spiritual dangers.

While the physical manifestations of angelic intervention may be less evident, their spiritual protection is as real and potent as ever. For instance, in the face of growing secularism and spiritual apathy, true Christians find the strength and motivation to remain steadfast, often attributing their spiritual resilience to unseen heavenly assistance.

The Necessity of this Protection

But why is such protection indispensable? The Scriptures reveal the existence of malevolent spirit creatures hell-bent on leading mankind astray. These are not figments of imagination but real entities with wicked intentions. To understand the gravity of the threat they pose, we must explore their origins, objectives, and strategies.

Wicked Spirit Creatures: Their Origin and Motive

Who are these dangerous spirit creatures, and where did they come from? Originally, all of Jehovah's spirit creations were perfect, reflecting His righteousness. However, a particular angel coveted worship that belonged exclusively to Jehovah, leading him to deceive the first human couple, Adam and Eve. This angel became known as Satan, meaning "Resister." Other angels, seduced by selfish desires, joined him in rebellion, eventually becoming known as demons. Their primary objective is to divert worship from Jehovah and lead humanity astray.

The Subtle Strategies of the Adversary

To recognize the danger posed by these wicked spirits, it's essential to understand their tactics. They employ a range of strategies from blatant temptations to subtle deceptions, designed to erode our spiritual defenses.

Why the Protection of Angels Is a Comfort

Given the formidable spiritual threats posed by wicked spirit creatures, the protective role of faithful angels becomes even more critical. They serve as Jehovah's instruments, fortifying us against the relentless onslaught of the Adversary. Knowing that these powerful, righteous angels are actively safeguarding us should fill our hearts with immense gratitude and comfort. In a world increasingly under the influence of malevolent spiritual entities, this divine protection is indispensable for our spiritual well-being.

Guardians Against Spiritual Harm

The angels' protective role isn't merely about averting physical dangers but, more importantly, shielding us from spiritual harm. In an era marked by skepticism, spiritual apathy, and increasing distance from Scriptural truths, the malevolent designs of the Adversary become all the more pronounced. Whether it's the allure of secular philosophies, the seduction of materialism, or the subtle undermining of Scriptural principles, Satan employs a multifaceted strategy to erode our faith. However, the protective hand of Jehovah's angels ensures that we're not left defenseless in this spiritual warfare. *Their interventions, though unseen, manifest in our ability to discern falsehoods, resist temptations, and hold fast to our faith despite external pressures.*

Dangers Beyond the Visible

Understanding that the real threat extends beyond the physical realm is crucial. Ephesians 6:12 reminds us, "For our struggle is not against flesh and blood, but against the rulers, against the authorities, against the cosmic powers of this darkness, against evil, spiritual forces in the heavens." This verse underscores the multifaceted spiritual warfare raging around us, emphasizing the necessity of divine protection.

Embracing Our Spiritual Armor

To withstand these attacks, we must not only rely on Jehovah's protection but also play our part. The subsequent verses in Ephesians chapter 6 detail the spiritual armor available to us – truth, righteousness, readiness, faith, salvation, and the word of God. Each element fortifies a specific aspect of our spiritual defenses, ensuring comprehensive protection against the Adversary's schemes.

Embracing Angelic Protection

As we navigate the spiritual minefield of Satan's world, the protection and guidance provided by Jehovah's angels are invaluable. Recognizing their role, however, should also inspire us to be proactive in our spiritual journey. Regular study of the Scriptures, fervent prayer, and active participation in the Christian congregation fortify our defenses, ensuring we remain steadfast in our faith. The psalmist's assurance that "The angel of Jehovah encamps around those who fear him and delivers them" should not only bring comfort but also motivate us to draw closer to Jehovah, confident that in doing so, we position ourselves securely under the protective watch of His mighty angels. We should mention again that we do not each individually have a guardian angel. They can protect an individual Christian if this benefits the outworking of God's will and purpose. However, angelic protect is composite in that it applies to God's people as a whole.

Satan's Substantial Success in Turning People Away

One cannot overstate Satan's effectiveness in drawing people away from the worship of Jehovah. His influence began in the Garden of Eden, subtly planting seeds of doubt in Eve's mind and successfully getting her and Adam to rebel against God. From that point on, a pattern emerged. Throughout history, under Satan's guidance, humanity has veered away from true worship, embracing falsehoods and immoral practices that directly oppose Jehovah's standards. Humanity's deviation from God's path culminated in the days of Noah when wickedness was so rampant that Jehovah decided to cleanse the earth.

The Angelic Descent: From Heavenly Servants to Earthly Tempters

The pre-Flood era saw a unique and unprecedented act of rebellion. Certain angels, beguiled by the allure of human women, abandoned their heavenly duties and posts. By materializing in human form, they took for themselves human wives, a direct violation of their divine nature and the purpose for which they were created. These actions led to the birth of the Nephilim, hybrid offspring described as "mighty ones of old times, the men of fame." (Genesis 6:4, UASV) These offspring further accelerated the moral decay, filling the earth with violence.

Surviving the Deluge: The Demons' Forced Retreat

As Jehovah decided to cleanse the earth through a global flood, these angels faced a predicament. Being inherently spirit creatures, they couldn't perish in the floodwaters. They had to abandon their physical, human forms and retreat to the spirit realm, thereby admitting their failure and rebellion. However, their departure from the earth was not a return to their previous honored state. Instead, it was a shameful acknowledgment of their rebellion.

The Outcast State of the Demons

Upon their return to heaven, these fallen angels found themselves in a significantly altered status. No longer were they honored members of Jehovah's family. Instead, they were outcasts, rebels who had aligned themselves with Satan in opposition to God. Peter's writings offer a glimpse into their degraded state, suggesting they were "thrown into Tartarus" and "delivered into chains of dense darkness" (2 Peter 2:4, UASV).

However, their confinement to the spirit realm did not strip them of all influence. Despite their inability to materialize in the flesh, their malevolent influence persisted. Their goal, much like their ruler Satan, was to mislead and turn as many away from Jehovah as possible.

The Pervasive Influence of Demons in Our World

Today, these demons, under Satan's rulership, exert substantial control over the world. Their methodologies are insidious. As Paul warned the Corinthians, we are not ignorant of their designs. They employ strategies tailored to exploit human weaknesses, spreading falsehoods to mislead people away from Jehovah. They stand behind false religions, ideologies, and philosophies that challenge or twist Scriptural truths, seeking always to draw worship away from Jehovah and to sow discord among His followers.

Protecting Ourselves from These Wicked Spirits

Recognizing their influence is the first step to resisting it. Jehovah, in His wisdom, has provided us with the necessary tools to discern and counteract their malicious intents. Regular study of the Scriptures, ardent prayers, association with the congregation, and a keen awareness of their tactics offer protection against their influences. As spiritual creatures, their warfare is inherently spiritual, targeting our faith, our beliefs, and our relationship with Jehovah. Thus, our defense must also be spiritual. Donning the full armor of God, as described in Ephesians 6:11-18, equips us to stand firm against their onslaughts.

The demons, once faithful angels, chose a path of rebellion, leading them to a fallen state. Today, they, alongside Satan, strive to turn hearts and minds away from Jehovah. However, armed with Scriptural knowledge and Jehovah's backing, we can resist their influences, remaining steadfast in our faith and loyalty to our Creator.

Demons: Masters of Deception

From the dawn of human history, demons have been relentless in their efforts to mislead us. These fallen angels, now following the lead of Satan, craftily employ a range of strategies to divert humans from the path of truth, righteousness, and a close relationship with Jehovah.

Spiritism: A Portal to the Demonic

What is Spiritism? Spiritism is the belief or doctrine that the spirits of the dead, surviving after the mortal life, can and do communicate with the living, especially through a person (a medium) particularly susceptible to their influence. This practice, which can include séances, channeling, and other forms of communication with spirits, opens a direct portal to demonic influences.

The Scriptures are explicit in their condemnation of spiritism. Leviticus 19:31 warns: "Do not turn to mediums or necromancers; do not seek them out, and so make yourselves unclean by them." Engaging in spiritistic practices or even dabbling in them exposes one to deceptive spirits who are eager to mislead and exploit.

Divination: The Forbidden Forecast

Defining Divination: Divination is the practice of seeking to gain insight or foretell future events through supernatural means. This could include practices such as reading tea leaves, interpreting omens, using tarot cards, or even consulting horoscopes.

Why Should We Steer Clear of Divination? God's Word is clear in its stance on divination. Deuteronomy 18:10-12 states, "There shall not be found among you anyone who practices divination or tells fortunes or interprets omens, or a sorcerer or a charmer or a medium or a necromancer or one who inquires of the dead, for whoever does these things is an abomination to Jehovah." The reason is clear: Divination often involves contacting or being influenced by demonic spirits, who are intent on misleading and drawing individuals away from the true God.

The Perils of Communicating with the Dead

Attempting to communicate with the departed is not only futile but also perilous. The dead, according to Ecclesiastes 9:5, "know nothing." Hence, any perceived communication from the dead is, in reality, a facade orchestrated by demons. By pretending to be deceased loved ones, these wicked spirits foster false beliefs about the nature of death and exploit the grieving, leading them further from Scriptural truth.

Additionally, seeking out the dead diminishes one's reliance on Jehovah and His Word for guidance and comfort. Why seek counsel from the deceased, whose knowledge is now null, when we can approach the Creator, who possesses infinite wisdom and understanding?

Triumphant Tales: Overcoming the Fear of Demons

Countless individuals, once ensnared by demonic practices and plagued by a palpable fear of malevolent spirits, have found freedom and peace in Jehovah. By immersing themselves in Scriptural truths, adopting a rigorous routine of prayer, and associating with God's people, they have managed to break free from the chains of demonism.

Acts 19:19-20 records a poignant moment where many who had previously practiced magic brought their scrolls and publicly burned them. Their bold act not only signified their clean break from demonic influences but also served as a powerful testimony of their newfound faith.

Demons, with their myriad deceptive tactics, pose a genuine spiritual threat. Spiritism, divination, and any attempts to communicate with the dead are gateways to their influence. However, with Jehovah's guidance, as found in the Scriptures, and a determined heart, one can resist and overcome these malevolent forces, finding true freedom and peace in the arms of our Creator.

The Battle Against Wicked Spirit Forces: A Comprehensive Strategy

The spiritual warfare waged by wicked spirit forces is relentless. However, Jehovah has provided believers with the tools and strategies to resist and overcome these malevolent entities. Engaging effectively in this spiritual warfare necessitates understanding the enemy, strengthening our faith, and adopting spiritual disciplines and habits that fortify us against demonic onslaughts.

Building an Impenetrable Fortress: Strengthening Our Faith

The Importance of Faith: Faith is not merely an intellectual assent to Scriptural truths; it is an unwavering trust in Jehovah and His promises. As Ephesians 6:16 states, faith acts as a "shield," quenching "all the flaming darts of the evil one."

Delving Deep into God's Word: Romans 10:17 reminds us that "faith comes from hearing, and hearing through the word of Christ." Regular, meditative reading of the Scriptures, not just superficial perusal, nourishes our soul, reinforces our convictions, and strengthens our faith. The Bible is Jehovah's communication to humanity, filled with accounts of His faithfulness, power, and love. By consistently immersing ourselves in it, we bolster our faith and resilience against wicked spirit forces.

Prayer - A Line of Communication: Prayer isn't just a ritual; it's a lifeline. It's our direct line of communication with Jehovah, where we express our fears, anxieties, gratitude, and requests. Through prayer, we draw strength from Jehovah, seeking His guidance, protection, and wisdom in combating wicked spirits. As Philippians 4:6-7 encourages, by making our requests known to God through prayer, His peace will guard our hearts and minds.

Steps to Resist Wicked Spirits

Avoiding Spiritistic Practices: Deuteronomy 18:10-12 offers a stark warning against engaging in practices that open doorways to demonic influences. This includes divination, sorcery, consulting with the dead, and more. To resist wicked spirits effectively, it's essential to avoid such practices entirely and eliminate any associated items or paraphernalia.

Wearing the Full Armor of God: Ephesians 6:11-17 provides a detailed description of the spiritual armor believers must wear. This includes the belt of truth, breastplate of righteousness, shoes of the gospel of peace, shield of faith, helmet of salvation, and the sword of the Spirit, which is God's Word. Each component of this armor serves a distinct purpose in defending against specific tactics of the devil and his demons.

Association with Fellow Believers: Hebrews 10:24-25 emphasizes the importance of not forsaking the assembling of believers. Fellowship provides mutual encouragement, accountability, and spiritual support, essential in the fight against wicked spirit forces. Through collective worship, study, and prayer, believers can draw strength from one another, united in their shared purpose and faith.

Assurance of Victory in Spiritual Warfare

Jehovah has not left us defenseless in this spiritual battle. The Scriptures offer numerous assurances of Jehovah's protection and the ultimate victory of His faithful servants over wicked spirit forces.

Jehovah's Superiority: Isaiah 40:22-26 highlights the unmatched greatness and power of Jehovah compared to the entirety of creation, including wicked spirit forces. His omnipotence guarantees that those who rely on Him will never be overcome by malevolent entities.

Christ's Triumph Over Wicked Spirits: Colossians 2:15 describes how Jesus, through His death and resurrection, disarmed the rulers and authorities (referring to wicked spirit forces) and put them to open shame by triumphing over them. This victory ensures that believers, as co-heirs with Christ, share in this triumph.

The Promised Outcome: Revelation 20:10 prophesies the ultimate fate of Satan and his demons – eternal torment in the lake of fire. This ensures that these wicked spirits have a limited time frame to operate and will soon face their impending doom.

CHAPTER 14 Do We Have Our Own Guardian Angels?

Psalm 91:11 Updated American Standard Version (UASV)

¹¹ For he will command **his angels concerning you** to guard you in all your ways.

The Bible doesn't explicitly state that each person has a guardian angel watching over them. Jesus did mention, "See that you do not despise one of these little ones [His followers], for... their angels in heaven... see the face of my Father who is in heaven." (Matthew 18:10) This suggests angels are interested in His disciples, but it doesn't guarantee each believer has a personal angel. Even if we're devoted in faith, we shouldn't expect an angel to shield us from all challenges.

But does this mean angels don't assist people? Not necessarily. As Psalm 91:11 points out, God directs His angels to guard us. Many believers feel they have a protective angel guiding them. Some experts, like S. Edward Tesh and Walter D. Zorn, believe angels guard people but not as "personal guardian" angels. The extent of angelic involvement in our lives remains a mystery. However, it's always good to show gratitude to God for any support we believe we've received. - Colossians 3:15; James 1:17, 18.

How Might Angels Help Us?

Angels, faithful to God, are curious about human actions and are dedicated to fulfilling God's plans. When God created the world, angels celebrated. (Job 38:4, 7) They've always been fascinated by human events (1 Pet. 1:11-12). The Bible contains many instances where God used angels to achieve His goals, including protecting His followers. (Psalm 34:7) S. Edward Tesh and Walter D. Zorn mentioned various occasions when angels acted as God's messengers, brought specific directives, intervened in wars, or offered protection.

For instance, angels shielded Lot in Sodom (Genesis 19) and closed the lion's mouths to save Daniel (Dan 6:22). - The College Press NIV Commentary (Joplin, MO: College Press, 1999), 180.

Angels Were Used in the First Century

There were specific times when God's angels intervened in the activities of the early Christian congregation to carry out God's will and purposes. For example:

Acts 8:26-31 Updated American Standard Version (UASV)

Philip and the Ethiopian Eunuch

²⁶ **But <u>an angel</u> of the Lord spoke to Philip saying**, "Get up and go south to the road that descends from Jerusalem to Gaza." (This is a desert road.) ²⁷ And he rose and went. And there was an Ethiopian, a eunuch, a court official of Candace, queen of the Ethiopians, who was in charge of all her treasure; who had come to worship in Jerusalem, ²⁸ and he was returning and sitting in his chariot, and was reading the prophet Isaiah. ²⁹ And the Spirit said to Philip, "Go over and join this chariot." ³⁰ So Philip ran to him and heard him reading Isaiah the prophet and asked, "Do you understand what you are reading?" ³¹ And he said, "How can I, unless someone guides me?" And he invited Philip to come up and sit with him. ³² Now the passage of the Scripture that he was reading was this:

"He was led as a sheep to slaughter
and like a lamb before its shearer is silent,
so he opens not his mouth.

Acts 10:3-5 Updated American Standard Version (UASV)

³ About the ninth hour of the day² he saw clearly in a vision **an <u>angel</u> of God** come in and say to him, "Cornelius." ⁴ And he stared at him, terrified, and asked, "What is it, Lord?" And he said to him, "Your prayers and your alms have ascended as a memorial before

---

² That is, about 3:00 p.m.

God. ⁵ And now send men to Joppa and bring one Simon who is called Peter.

Acts 12:1-11 Updated American Standard Version (UASV)

James Killed and Peter Imprisoned

12 About that time Herod the king laid violent hands on some who belonged to the congregation. ² And he killed James the brother of John with a sword. ³ And when he saw that it was pleasing to the Jews, he proceeded to arrest Peter also. Now this was during the feast of Unleavened Bread. ⁴ And when he had seized him, he put him in prison, delivering him over to four squads of soldiers³ to guard him, intending after the Passover to bring him out to the people. ⁵ So Peter was kept in prison, but earnest prayer for him was made to God by the congregation.

Peter Is Miraculously Rescued

⁶ Now when Herod was about to bring him out, that night Peter was sleeping bound with two chains between two soldiers, and guards in front of the door were keeping watch over the prison. ⁷ And look, an angel of the Lord stood next to him, and a light shone in the cell. He struck Peter on the side and woke him, saying, "Get up quickly." And the chains fell off his hands. ⁸ And the angel said to him, "Gird yourself and put on your sandals!" And he did so. And he said to him, "Wrap your cloak around you and follow me!" ⁹ And he went out and followed, and he did not know that what took place through the angel was real, but thought he was seeing a vision. ¹⁰ When they had passed the first and second guard, they came to the iron gate that leads into the city, which opened for them by itself; and they went out and went along one street, and immediately the angel departed from him. ¹¹ When Peter came to himself, he said, "Now I am sure that the Lord has sent his angel and rescued me from the hand of Herod and from all that the Jewish people were expecting."⁴

---

³ Lit *quaternions*; a quaternion was composed of four soldiers; so, four shifts of four soldiers

⁴ Edward D. Andrews, ed., *Updated American Standard Version*, trans. Edward D. Andrews (Cambridge, OH: Christian Publishing House, 2022), Ac 12:1–11.

INTRODUCTION TO OLD TESTAMENT TEXTUAL CRITICISM

Why Did the Disciples Say: "It is his angel"?

Acts 12:12-15 Updated American Standard Version (UASV)

[12] When he realized this, he went to the house of Mary, the mother of John whose other name was Mark, where many were gathered together and were praying. [13] And when he knocked at the door of the gateway, a servant girl named Rhoda came to answer. [14] And recognizing Peter's voice, in her joy she did not open the gate but ran in and reported that Peter was standing at the gate. [15] They said to her, "You are out of your mind!" But she kept insisting that it was so, and they kept saying, "**It is his angel!**"

Context of Acts 12:15

Peter was arrested by Herod, who had already executed James. The disciples probably assumed Peter had met the same fate. However, while guarded by soldiers, an angel miraculously freed Peter from his chains and guided him out of prison. When he comprehended the situation, Peter remarked, "The Lord sent his angel to rescue me from Herod." — Acts 12:1-11.

After escaping, Peter headed straight to Mary's house, where several disciples had gathered. He knocked, and Rhoda, hearing his voice, ran to the others in excitement, leaving Peter at the door. The disciples, in disbelief, thought: "It is his angel." — Acts 12:12-15.

So, what did the disciples mean by "It is his angel"?

Given their Jewish heritage, they were familiar with numerous accounts where angels, taking human form, aided God's people. Jacob referenced "the angel who has redeemed me from all evil." (Gen. 48:16) Jesus, discussing a child, stated: "Their angels in heaven always see the face of my Father in heaven." (Matt. 18:10) Additionally, other angelic encounters are documented in the book of Acts.

Thus, instead of assuming Peter's spirit was at the gate post-execution, they believed an angel representing or resembling Peter might be outside, given the miraculous nature of their times and previous biblical incidents involving angels.

Acts 12:15 Young's Literal Translation (YLT)

¹⁵ and they said unto her, `Thou art mad;' and she was confidently affirming [it] to be so, and they said, `**It is his messenger;'**

The Young's Literal Translation translates the Greek word (angelos) as "messenger" rather than the common term "angel". This hints at the possibility that the Jews of that time might have believed each servant of God had a unique guardian angel.

> Many Jews believed in the notion of an angel who was closely associated with a person and could even take on that person's appearance. Note the book of Tobit, where the angel Raphael took on the disguise of Azarias (a relative of Tobit's) and became a guide for Tobit's son, Tobias (Tobit 5:4–16). Jesus himself spoke of angels associated with children: "See that you do not look down on one of these little ones. For I tell you that their angels in heaven always see the face of my Father in heaven" (Matt. 18:10). This led to a belief in the church about angels assigned to people for their lifetimes and who from time to time intervene on their behalf.[5]

However, this perspective isn't directly supported in the Bible's inspired and inerrant sections. When the disciples told Rhoda, "It is his angel," they might have mistakenly believed that an angelic figure, representing Peter, was at the door. This isn't a mistake in the Bible itself but could be a potential misconception of the disciples that Luke accurately recorded. It isn't a doctrinal statement but a historical account.

Guardian Angels: Fact or Fiction?

If every believer has a guardian angel, why are some saved while others face tragedy? Throughout history, countless Christians have

---

[5] Clinton E. Arnold, *Zondervan Illustrated Bible Backgrounds Commentary: John, Acts.*, vol. 2 (Grand Rapids, MI: Zondervan, 2002), 329.

suffered due to various adversities, even after seeking divine intervention. So, why didn't their guardian angels intervene?

While angels might be concerned about our well-being, their primary focus is on our spiritual growth. Paul even questions, "Aren't all angels ministering spirits sent to serve those who will inherit salvation?" (Heb. 1:14). God might occasionally provide physical help, but spiritual guidance has everlasting impacts.

Many tales of angelic interventions seem trivial. Stories range from angels assisting in everyday chores to finding parking spots. Some accounts, like expecting angels to prevent traffic tickets, are as far-fetched as tales of Santa Claus.

God's angels won't go against His Word. Thus, tales of angels that don't align with the Scriptures should be viewed with skepticism. Paul even warns against those preaching a gospel different from the original, even if an "angel" conveys it (Galatians 1:6-8).

The Bible never instructs us to call upon angels. Jesus, in his example prayer, directs us towards God, saying, "Pray in this way: 'Our Father in heaven…'" (Matthew 6:9). Paul also guides believers to seek God in times of distress and gratitude (Philippians 4:6).

Understanding Angels in the Bible

The Bible specifically mentions only two angels by name: Michael and Gabriel. (Dan. 12:1; Lu 1:26) This limited naming indicates that each angel is a distinct spirit entity, just as every human being is unique. However, the absence of more names is intentional. God wanted to ensure that his followers don't place undue importance or admiration on angels, an attention the angels themselves wouldn't desire. For instance, when Jacob inquired an angel's name, the angel chose not to reveal it. (Gen. 32:29) Similarly, an angel introduced himself to Joshua as the "commander of the army of Jehovah" rather than by name. (Josh.5:14) When Samson's father inquired an angel's name, the angel responded cryptically: "Why do you ask my name, seeing it is wonderful?" (Judges 13:17, 18) It's clear: God's angels prioritize His glory above their own.

God's Protection Through Angels

At times, God has protected His followers, both physically and spiritually, either miraculously or via angelic intervention. Yet, miraculous interventions, even in biblical accounts, were rare. Throughout the vast span of Biblical history, there are many instances or even centuries without any recorded miraculous event.

Psalm 91:11, UASV: 11 He promises protection for those truly devoted to Him, saying he will "command his angels concerning you to guard you in all your ways."

While God did occasionally provide physical protection to preserve the lineage leading to the Messiah, many devoted servants faced immense hardships, from imprisonment to torture, even death. Despite these physical adversities, their spiritual integrity remained unshaken, thanks to God's spiritual shield.

Psalm 91:1-2, UASV: 91 "He who dwells in the secret place* of the Most High will rest in the shadow of the Almighty. 2 I will declare about Jehovah, 'He is my refuge and my fortress, my God in whom I trust.'" *or shelter

Psalm 91 emphasizes spiritual safeguarding. The "secret place of the Most High" symbolizes a protective spiritual haven. This refuge remains hidden or secretive because it's inaccessible to non-believers or insincere followers. While God offers this protection to everyone, it doesn't guarantee physical safety. But spiritual protection is always assured. It's also vital to note that Psalm 91 doesn't advocate reckless behavior.

Michael, the Archangel

Michael, the archangel, operates directly under Jesus Christ. (Matt 13:41; 16:27; 24:31; 2 Thess. 1:7; 1 Pet. 3:22; Rev. 19:14-16) While Michael guards God's devoted followers collectively, he isn't an individual's personal guardian. Yet, he designates angels to protect believers from malicious angels. For instance, a loyal angel once annihilated 185,000 Assyrian soldiers overnight. Without this protection, rogue angels could decimate God's followers swiftly. However, these angels don't shield us from human flaws or worldly evils.

CHAPTER 15 Is There a Difference Between Immortality and Eternal Life?

1 Corinthians 15:54 Updated American Standard Version (UASV)

⁵⁴ When the perishable puts on the imperishable, and the mortal puts on **immortality**, then shall come to pass the saying that is written: "Death is swallowed up in victory."

John 3:16 Updated American Standard Version (UASV)

¹⁶ For God so loved the world that he gave his only begotten Son, in order that whoever believes in him will not be destroyed but have **eternal life**.

IMMORTALITY: (ἄφθαρτος aphthartos) immortal, imperishable, indestructible, cannot be destroyed, so, of course, it means lasting forever

ETERNAL LIFE: (ζωὴν αἰώνιον zōē aiōnion) means eternal, an unlimited duration.

This is not really semantics because, if taken literally, immortality means the being is imperishable and indestructible, which means the being cannot be destroyed. The Greek word translated "immortality" (ἀφθαρσία aphtharsia) is formed from the negative "a" and from (θάνατος thanatos), meaning "death." Therefore, the basic sense of immortality is 'without death.' It has always been that only God was indestructible (Psalm 36:9; 90:1-2). The Son, who is "the radiance of his glory and the exact representation of his nature," is described as "the blessed and only Sovereign, the King of those who reign as kings and Lord of those who rule as lords, **the one who alone possesses immortality**." (Hebrews 1:3; 1 Timothy 6:15-16) No creature can take

The Father or the Son's life as they are immortal, which makes them different from humans or angels, that are destructible.

Even Michael the archangel, the highest-ranking angel and the second most powerful being there, is, aside from God, destructible. That is, he can be destroyed. So, the question that now begs to be asked will everyone who receives eternal life be immortal? I highly doubt that. Those that go to heaven will receive immortality, which encompasses eternal life, and those on earth will receive eternal life. However, they can still be destroyed, which is clear from what will happen to some after the thousand-year reign of Christ when some will be tempted by Satan and receive the Second Death from which there is no resurrection. Even though Adam and Eve were created to live forever, they were not immortal. So, immortality does encompass the sense of eternal life, but it is beyond that as it implies more than the fact that the person having immortality will live forever. It is connected with incorruption, which is imperishable, indestructible, cannot be destroyed, and cannot die.

1 Corinthians 15:53-55 Updated American Standard Version (UASV)
[53] For this perishable must put on the imperishable, and this mortal must put on **immortality**. [54] When the perishable puts on the **imperishable**, and the mortal puts on **immortality**, then shall come to pass the saying that is written:

"Death is swallowed up in victory."
[55] "O death, where is your victory?
O death, where is your sting?"

However, the Bible does not offer us many insights into what life will be like for those who receive immortality. As was said above, Adam and Eve possessed eternal life. And we know that they had to eat food and drink water to maintain life. It can be inferred that if, hypothetically, they stopped eating and drinking water, they would die, and they would experience corruption, even though they possessed eternal life. (Genesis 2:9, 15, 16) There is nothing within the Scriptures that would suggest that those who will receive immortal life in heaven with spirit bodies will need to consume something to sustain their eternal life. Thus, immortals are not subject to death. When they receive their spirit body, they will be imperishable, receiving incorruptibility. (Compare 2 Corinthians 5:1; Revelation 20:6) Thus, immortality involves eternal life but also deathlessness, unable to die, cannot be destroyed, while eternal life here on earth does not involve these things.

CHAPTER 16 The Cosmic Conflict: Truth vs. Lies

At the very heart of the Christian experience lies a profound and tumultuous battle, one that has been waged for millennia. This battle is not merely a dispute among humans or a fleeting cultural trend. It is a cosmic conflict between truth and lies, between divine teaching and the deceptions of demons. This battle is far-reaching, and its implications are eternal.

The Source of the Battle: The Rebellion in Heaven

Before humanity set foot on the earth, a significant event transpired in heaven that set the stage for this spiritual war. Scripture reveals that an angel, named Lucifer, allowed pride to fill his heart. He sought to place himself above Jehovah, the almighty Creator (Isaiah 14:12-15; Ezekiel 28:12-17). This rebellion led to his expulsion from heaven, and he became known as Satan, meaning "adversary."

Revelation 12:7-9 tells us, "And war broke out in heaven: Michael and his angels battled with the dragon, and the dragon and its angels battled but they did not prevail, nor was a place found for them any longer in heaven. So down the great dragon was hurled, the original serpent, the one called Devil and Satan, who is misleading the entire inhabited earth."

The Battlefield: The Minds and Hearts of Humanity

Upon his expulsion, Satan turned his attention to humanity, eager to drag them into his rebellious scheme. The Garden of Eden was the initial scene of his deceit, where he cunningly twisted Jehovah's words and led Adam and Eve to sin (Genesis 3:1-5). By doing so, Satan introduced not just sin but also a powerful narrative: the lie that humans could decide for themselves what is right and wrong, independent of their Creator.

Throughout history, Satan and his demons have continually promoted lies to draw individuals away from the truths found in Scripture. Christians are in the thick of this battle, for their faith makes them prime targets. As Paul wrote to the Ephesians, "For our struggle is not against flesh and blood, but against the rulers, against the authorities, against the powers of this dark world and against the spiritual forces of evil in the heavenly realms" (*Ephesians 6:12*).

Weapons of the Enemy: Lies, Half-truths, and Deception

Satan's primary weapons are not physical but ideological. Lies, half-truths, and cunning deceptions are his preferred tools. He "masquerades as an angel of light" (*2 Corinthians 11:14*), which means he can make falsehoods appear attractive or even righteous.

One prevalent lie is the denial of Jehovah's sovereignty. By promoting the idea that God does not care, is absent, or is powerless, Satan seeks to discourage trust in Jehovah. Another lie is the perversion of moral values, leading individuals to believe that what is wrong in God's eyes can somehow be justified by human reasoning.

The Defense: Armor of God and Divine Truth

Amidst these assaults, Jehovah has not left Christians defenseless. Paul provides guidance on how to resist the devil's schemes in *Ephesians 6:13-17*. He encourages believers to put on the full armor of God: the belt of truth, the breastplate of righteousness, the shield of faith, the helmet of salvation, and the sword of the Spirit, which is the word of God.

Hebrews 4:12 reminds us that the word of God is "alive and active. Sharper than any double-edged sword, it penetrates even to dividing soul and spirit, joints and marrow; it judges the thoughts and attitudes of the heart." Through diligent study and application of the Scriptures, Christians can discern truth from falsehood and withstand demonic influences.

The Ultimate Victory: Jehovah's Promise

It would be naive to think that this spiritual warfare will rage indefinitely. Jehovah has set a time when He will intervene, judging Satan and his demons, casting them into eternal destruction, a fate mentioned in *Revelation 20:10*.

While this cosmic battle ensues, it is vital to recognize that Jehovah's victory is assured. *1 John 4:4* assures Christians: "You are from God, little children, and have overcome them; because greater is He who is in you than he who is in the world." This divine guarantee serves as a beacon of hope, ensuring believers that while they might face trials and tribulations now, they are on the winning side.

Perseverance in Truth: The Christian's Role

Every Christian plays a pivotal role in this battle. By living in accordance with Jehovah's teachings and rejecting the world's falsehoods, they serve as shining beacons of truth in a darkened world. They must remain vigilant, always ready to "demolish arguments and every pretension that sets itself up against the knowledge of God, and take captive every thought to make it obedient to Christ" (*2 Corinthians 10:5*).

By upholding the truth of Scripture and living righteously, Christians not only protect themselves but also bear witness to others, guiding them towards the path of salvation.

Paul's Dualistic Worldview: Flesh vs. Spirit

A profound understanding of the Apostle Paul's writings reveals his emphasis on the antagonism between two opposing forces: the flesh and the spirit. For Paul, the tension between these two forces was not merely a theological concept but a lived reality, intricately woven into the daily experiences of believers.

The Flesh: Earthly Desires and Weakness

Paul often uses the term "flesh" (*sarx* in Greek) to describe the fallen human nature, which is inherently weak and susceptible to sin. In his letter to the Romans, Paul laments the struggles he faces due to the desires of the flesh, expressing, "For I do not do the good I want to do, but the evil I do not want to do—this I keep on doing" (*Romans 7:19*). This struggle indicates that the flesh is in constant opposition to the righteous desires of a believer, always pulling them towards worldly temptations and away from God.

The Spirit: Divine Guidance and Power

Conversely, the spirit represents the divine influence in a believer's life, guiding and empowering them to live righteously. This is not an internal human spirit but the influence of God's Spirit through the inspired Word of God. Paul highlights this in his letter to the Galatians, stating, "But the fruit of the Spirit is love, joy, peace, forbearance, kindness, goodness, faithfulness, gentleness, and self-control" (*Galatians 5:22-23*). The presence of these qualities signifies a life aligned with the spirit, triumphing over the desires of the flesh.

Understanding "the Faith": Paul's Definition

For Paul, "the faith" was not a vague or nebulous concept. It referred to the body of Christian beliefs, the teachings of Jesus Christ as passed down through his disciples, and the inspired letters of apostles like Paul himself. "The faith" encapsulated the core tenets of Christianity and served as a foundation upon which believers could anchor their lives.

In his letter to the Corinthians, Paul emphasizes the importance of maintaining the purity of "the faith," warning against those who might corrupt it: "For if someone comes to you and preaches a Jesus other than the Jesus we preached, or if you receive a different spirit from the Spirit you received, or a different gospel from the one you accepted, you put up with it easily enough" (*2 Corinthians 11:4*). This demonstrates Paul's fervent commitment to safeguarding the integrity of Christian teachings.

Casualties in the Battle: The Consequences of Deception

Paul was acutely aware that the battle between truth and lies had real and lasting consequences. Those deceived by falsehoods risked spiritual death – a state of eternal separation from Jehovah.

Paul warns Timothy about such dangers, emphasizing the importance of adhering to the teachings of Scripture: "O Timothy, guard the deposit entrusted to you. Avoid the irreverent babble and contradictions of what is falsely called 'knowledge,' for by professing it some have swerved from the faith" (*1 Timothy 6:20-21*). These words paint a stark picture: deviation from the truth leads to spiritual ruin.

Teachings of Demons: The Dark Puppeteers

Paul was unequivocal about the source behind the deceptive teachings that sought to lead believers astray. Satan, the chief adversary of Jehovah and humanity, operates through his legions of fallen angels or demons, sowing seeds of confusion, doubt, and falsehood.

Paul explicitly warns about such demonic influences in his letters. To Timothy, he writes, "The Spirit clearly says that in later times some will abandon the faith and follow deceiving spirits and things taught by demons" (*1 Timothy 4:1*). This passage reveals the nefarious objective of these spirits: to divert believers from the path of righteousness, using deceptive teachings as their primary weapon.

Paul's letters provide a profound insight into the spiritual warfare that rages within and around every believer. He paints a vivid picture of the conflict between the flesh and the spirit, emphasizing the vital importance of adhering to "the faith." For Paul, the stakes are incredibly high. Those ensnared by the teachings of demons risk eternal separation from Jehovah. Yet, through the inspired Word of God and steadfast commitment to the truth, believers can navigate this tumultuous battle and secure their place in Jehovah's eternal kingdom.

The Deception in Eden: Satan's Lie to Eve

The Garden of Eden, often described as a paradise, was the scene of one of the most profound deceptions in human history. This deception, orchestrated by Satan, has had repercussions that echo to this day.

Satan's Lie: Doubting Jehovah's Words

When Satan, manifesting as a serpent, approached Eve, he cunningly asked, "Did God really say, 'You must not eat from any tree in the garden'?" (*Genesis 3:1*). Eve corrected him, noting that only the fruit from the tree of the knowledge of good and evil was forbidden. However, Satan boldly proclaimed, "You will not certainly die" (*Genesis 3:4*), directly contradicting Jehovah's explicit command.

This was more than a mere lie; it was a profound deception. Satan wasn't merely contradicting Jehovah; he was implying that Jehovah was withholding something good from Adam and Eve. He suggested that eating the fruit would make them "like God, knowing good and evil" (*Genesis 3:5*), insinuating that Jehovah's prohibition was a means of keeping them subjugated.

The Wickedness of the Lie

At its core, Satan's lie was so wicked because it questioned the very nature of Jehovah: His goodness, truthfulness, and love for His creation. Satan painted Jehovah as a deceptive ruler, hiding beneficial knowledge from humanity. By doing so, he introduced doubt into Eve's mind, causing her to question the benevolence of her Creator.

Challenging the Goodness and Sovereignty of God

Beyond the immediate lie, Satan's words were a broader challenge to Jehovah's character and sovereignty. By suggesting that Jehovah had ulterior motives, Satan was undermining God's position as a loving, just, and righteous Creator. This challenge wasn't just about a piece of fruit; it was an assault on the very foundation of humanity's relationship with their Creator.

The Earliest Teachings of Demons

The conversation between Satan and Eve in Eden marks the first instance where demonic teachings were introduced to humanity. Yet, the themes of these teachings – doubt, deception, and rebellion – are threads that run through the entire tapestry of human history.

Even today, many teachings and ideologies mirror Satan's initial deception. They question the validity of God's Word, challenge His goodness, or promote self-interest over divine command. In essence, modern falsehoods often echo the serpent's ancient whisper, "Did God really say...?"

The Consequences in Eden: Loss and Separation

The repercussions of heeding Satan's words were swift and devastating. By choosing to eat the forbidden fruit, Adam and Eve introduced sin into the world. This act led to their immediate spiritual death – a separation from Jehovah – and eventually to their physical death.

Beyond their personal loss, Adam and Eve's actions had broader consequences for all of humanity. Their descendants, including all of us today, inherited a sinful nature, leading to a world filled with pain, suffering, and death.

God's Truth and Redemption

While the events in Eden were undeniably tragic, they also served to highlight the truthfulness and faithfulness of Jehovah. What He had warned came to pass, proving that His words were neither deceptive nor misleading.

Moreover, Jehovah, in His infinite love and mercy, set into motion a plan for redemption shortly after the fall. He promised that a "seed" would come, referring to the Messiah, who would crush the serpent's head (*Genesis 3:15*). This prophecy pointed to Jesus Christ, who, through His sacrificial death, would offer salvation to all of humanity.

Even in the darkest moments of human history, Jehovah's truth shone brightly. Despite Satan's attempts to mar God's character, Jehovah's actions consistently proved His unchanging love, mercy, and righteousness.

The events in Eden, while heartbreaking, provide profound insights into the nature of the cosmic battle between truth and deception. Satan's lie to Eve wasn't a mere falsehood; it was an assault on Jehovah's character and sovereignty. Yet, even amidst the tragedy, Jehovah's truthfulness was evident. His promises, both of consequence and redemption, came to pass, showcasing His unwavering commitment to justice and love. As believers, reflecting on these events serves as a poignant reminder of the dangers of deception and the unchanging faithfulness of our Creator.

The Historical Influence of Demonic Teachings

From the earliest moments of human history, the teachings of demons have had a profound and often devastating impact on civilizations, societies, and individuals. These teachings, rooted in deception and opposition to Jehovah's truths, have manifested in various forms throughout the ages, influencing countless lives and shaping the course of history.

Centuries of Deception: The Far-reaching Impact

The efficacy of demonic teachings can be traced through the annals of history. From ancient pagan rituals, idolatries, and superstitions to more modern ideologies and philosophies that stand in stark contrast to Scriptural truths, the fingerprints of demonic influence are unmistakable.

Many ancient civilizations, such as the Egyptians, Babylonians, Greeks, and Romans, had pantheons filled with gods and goddesses. These deities, often appeased through elaborate rituals, sacrifices, and ceremonies, were manifestations of demonic influences, drawing people away from the worship of the one true God, Jehovah.

In later centuries, as Christianity began to spread, demonic teachings sought to infiltrate and corrupt the nascent faith. Heresies, schisms, and false doctrines emerged, leading many astray and causing divisions within the body of believers.

Modern Manifestations: The Contemporary Face of Deception

As the world has evolved, so too have the strategies of Satan and his demons. While the core objective remains – leading humanity away from Jehovah – the methods and mediums have adapted to fit the modern context.

1. **Secular Humanism:** One of the prevailing ideologies of the modern age, secular humanism places humanity at the center of all things, often sidelining or outright rejecting the idea of a divine Creator. This worldview, which prioritizes human reasoning over divine revelation, echoes the serpent's whisper in Eden: "You will be like God."

2. **Materialism:** In a world increasingly driven by consumerism, the pursuit of wealth, possessions, and temporal pleasures can easily become the primary focus of life. Such materialistic tendencies divert attention from spiritual matters, making it challenging for many to perceive the deeper, eternal truths of Scripture.

3. **Religious Syncretism:** In the name of tolerance and coexistence, some advocate for blending various religious beliefs and practices, diluting the purity of Scriptural teachings and creating a spiritual mishmash that lacks a firm foundation in truth.

4. **Moral Relativism:** The idea that there are no absolute truths, especially in the realm of morality and ethics, has gained traction in recent decades. By asserting that "truth" is subjective and can vary from person to person, moral relativism undermines the objective standards set forth in Scripture.

Satan's Current Activities: The Subtle Warfare

While the methods may vary, Satan's objectives remain consistent. He seeks to deceive, divide, and ultimately destroy humanity's relationship with Jehovah.

1. **Distraction:** One of Satan's most effective tactics in the modern age is simply to distract. With a plethora of entertainment, technologies, and daily demands, many individuals find little time for spiritual reflection, prayer, or Scripture study.
2. **Doubt:** Just as he did with Eve, Satan continues to sow seeds of doubt, causing individuals to question the authenticity of Scripture, the existence of Jehovah, or the relevance of faith in the contemporary world.
3. **Division:** Through the promotion of ideologies that are in direct opposition to Scriptural truths, Satan fosters divisions — both within the body of believers and between Christians and the broader world. These divisions can lead to conflict, misunderstanding, and alienation.
4. **Direct Opposition:** While subtlety is often his preferred method, Satan also operates through more overt opposition to Jehovah and His followers. This can manifest as persecution, discrimination, or open hostility towards those who uphold Scriptural truths.

The teachings of demons, while ancient in origin, continue to exert a significant influence in the modern world. Through a myriad of methods, both subtle and overt, Satan and his demons work tirelessly to divert humanity from the path of righteousness. Yet, by remaining grounded in the inspired Word of God and vigilant against the schemes of the enemy, believers can navigate this spiritual minefield, holding fast to the eternal truths revealed in Scripture.

The Power to Resist Demonic Teachings

While the influence of demonic teachings has been pervasive throughout history, it is essential to understand that individuals are not powerless against such deceptions. Jehovah has provided the means for believers to discern and resist falsehoods.

1. **The Inspired Word of God:** Scripture serves as the ultimate touchstone of truth. By regularly studying and meditating upon the Bible, believers can equip themselves with knowledge, fortifying their minds against deceptive teachings (*2 Timothy 3:16-17*).
2. **The Body of Believers:** The Christian community, or the Church, provides mutual encouragement, support, and accountability. Through collective worship, study, and fellowship, believers can strengthen one another in their faith and stand united against demonic influences (*Hebrews 10:24-25*).

Satan's Tactics Against Servants of God

Satan is acutely aware of those who serve Jehovah faithfully and often employs specific strategies to divert such individuals from their spiritual path.

1. **Persecution:** Throughout history, faithful servants of God have faced direct persecution, whether through societal

discrimination, governmental oppression, or even physical harm (*1 Peter 5:8-9*).

2. **Temptation:** Satan often presents seemingly attractive opportunities for servants of God to compromise their values, be it through wealth, power, or personal relationships (*James 1:14-15*).

3. **Doubt:** Much like his approach with Eve, Satan continues to introduce doubt into the minds of believers, making them question the veracity of Scripture or the goodness of Jehovah (*Genesis 3:1-5*).

Lies Since Eden: Satan's Continuous Deceptions

Post the Eden deception, Satan has woven a web of lies, each tailored to the cultural, societal, and personal contexts of various eras.

1. **Idolatry:** Throughout ancient times, Satan promoted the worship of false gods, leading people away from Jehovah.

2. **Self-Sufficiency:** The lie that humans can achieve true happiness, success, or salvation independent of Jehovah has persisted through the ages.

3. **Moral Relativity:** The idea that there are no objective moral truths, and that individuals can define their own "truths," is a modern manifestation of Satan's deception.

The Truth About Death and Future Hope

Contrary to many of Satan's lies regarding death and the afterlife, the Bible provides clear teachings. Death is described as a deep sleep, a state of unconsciousness (*Ecclesiastes 9:5*). However, Jehovah, in His love and mercy, has provided the hope of resurrection, a promise that the dead will be brought back to life (*John 5:28-29*). This resurrection provides believers with a profound hope for the future, either in a restored earthly paradise or in heaven.

The Results of Human Wisdom

When humanity relies solely on its wisdom, devoid of divine guidance, the results are often detrimental. Such reliance can lead to societal injustices, moral degradation, and spiritual emptiness. The Bible cautions that "There is a way that seems right to a man, but its end is the way to death" (*Proverbs 14:12*).

"Falsely Called Knowledge": Satan's Modern Deceptions

Throughout history, various ideologies and philosophies have been promoted as "knowledge," leading many away from Scriptural truths. Today, such deceptions might include certain scientific theories that contradict Scripture, secular philosophies that deny the existence of God, or religious teachings that deviate from biblical doctrine. The fruits of such "knowledge" are evident in societal confusion, moral decay, and a growing sense of spiritual emptiness. As Paul warned Timothy, this "falsely called knowledge" can make some deviate from the faith (*1 Timothy 6:20-21*).

While the teachings of demons and the lies of Satan are pervasive and multifaceted, Jehovah has provided believers with the tools to discern and resist such deceptions. By grounding themselves in Scripture, seeking communal support, and relying on divine wisdom, believers can navigate the challenges of this world, holding fast to eternal truths and hope.

Seekers of True Divine Teaching

In our age of spiritual pluralism, discerning who genuinely seeks divine teaching becomes a critical task. True seekers of divine instruction are not merely content with surface-level spirituality or rituals but deeply delve into the foundation of conservative

Christianity. This foundation is built upon the belief in the inspired and inerrant Word of God, which means every word of the Bible is divinely inspired and without error in its original manuscripts.

Conservative Christianity: Anchored in Truth

Conservative Christianity emphasizes a faithful, unyielding commitment to the Scriptures. These believers understand that the authors of the Bible wrote with clear intent, guided by the Holy Spirit, conveying divine truths for humanity. Unlike the liberal-moderate approach of the Historical-Critical Method, which is subjective and often doubts the supernatural elements of the Bible, the conservative, objective Historical-Grammatical Method seeks to understand the Bible based on the authors' original intent, historical context, and the plain meaning of the text. This method ensures a pure, undiluted understanding of divine teachings, free from human biases or reinterpretations.

Being Taught by God: A Comprehensive Experience

Being taught by Jehovah is not merely an intellectual exercise. It encompasses the following:

1. **Scriptural Study:** This involves diligently studying the Bible, seeking to understand its teachings, prophecies, commandments, and principles.

2. **Prayerful Meditation:** Beyond reading, believers commune with Jehovah through prayer, seeking His guidance, wisdom, and understanding.

3. **Application:** True divine teaching translates into action. Believers apply the principles learned from the Scriptures in their daily lives, reflecting the character of Christ in their thoughts, words, and deeds.

4. **Spiritual Discernment:** Through continuous engagement with the Scriptures, believers develop the ability to discern between truth and falsehood, ensuring they remain on the righteous path.

Satan's Blinding Tactics

Satan, the great deceiver, employs numerous strategies to blind humanity to the truths of Jehovah. As the Apostle Paul wrote to the Corinthians: "The god of this age has blinded the minds of unbelievers, so that they cannot see the light of the gospel that displays the glory of Christ, who is the image of God" (*2 Corinthians 4:4*). Furthermore, Paul warns against false apostles and deceitful workers who masquerade as apostles of Christ, noting that even Satan can masquerade as an angel of light (*2 Corinthians 11:13-15*).

Among Satan's blinding tactics are:

1. **False Doctrines:** Introducing teachings that deviate from the Scriptures, leading people into error.
2. **Worldly Distractions:** Bombarding individuals with materialistic desires, ambitions, and pursuits that divert their attention from spiritual matters.
3. **Moral Relativism:** Sowing confusion by promoting the idea that there are no absolute moral truths, leading to a decline in righteousness and a departure from God's standards.

Blessings from the Inerrant Word of God

For those who steadfastly cling to the inspired and inerrant Word of God, the blessings are manifold:

1. **Spiritual Growth:** Through regular engagement with the Scriptures, believers mature in their faith, developing a deeper understanding of Jehovah and His ways.

2. **Guidance:** The Bible provides direction for every aspect of life, ensuring that believers walk in righteousness and make decisions aligned with Jehovah's will.

3. **Protection:** Armed with Scriptural truths, believers can fend off the deceptive tactics of Satan, ensuring they remain on the path of salvation.

4. **Eternal Hope:** The Scriptures provide the assurance of salvation through Jesus Christ, offering believers the hope of eternal life in the presence of Jehovah.

5. **Inner Peace:** Grounded in the promises and teachings of the Bible, believers experience inner peace, knowing that they are in Jehovah's care and that all things work together for the good of those who love Him.

Conclusion

In a world awash with varied spiritual teachings and philosophies, the genuine seeker of divine instruction turns to the inspired and inerrant Word of God. Through conservative Christianity, believers anchor themselves in unchanging truths, protected from the blinding tactics of Satan. The blessings that flow from such unwavering commitment are profound, ensuring spiritual growth, divine guidance, and eternal hope.

Edward D. Andrews

GLOSSARY of Related Biblical Terms

Abyss

(Gr. *abussos*) It is a very deep place, which is rendered "the bottomless pit" in some versions (KJV). This is found the NT and refers to a place or condition, where Satan and his demons will be confined for a thousand years. (Rev. 20:1-3) Abaddon rules over the abyss (Rev. 9:11) The beast is of Satan's design and will rise from the abyss in the last days. (Rev. 11:7) The beat will go off into destruction. (Rev 17:8) It is used as times to refer to the grave as well.–Lu 8:31; Rom. 10:7; Rev. 20:3.

Angel

(Heb. *mălăk*; Gr. *angelos*) A supernatural spirit person who attends upon or serves as a messenger or worker for the Father and the Son. These spirit persons are far wiser and more powerful than humans but their power and knowledge is absolutely nothing in comparison to their Creator. (Ps. 103:20; Matt. 24:36; 1 Pet. 1:1-12) Angels have the power to be able to material in human form. (Gen. 18:1-2, 8, 20-22; 19:1-11; Josh. 5:13-15) Some of these angels became rebels. Jude tells us "the angels who did not keep to their own domain but deserted their proper dwelling place [heaven]" (1:6), to take on human form, and have relations that were contrary to nature with the "the daughters of man." (Gen 6:1-4; Dan. 7:9-10) The Bible intimates that these rebel angels were stripped of their power to take on human form, as you never hear of it taking place again after the Flood, only spirit possession thereafter. These disobedient angels are now "spirits in prison," who have been thrown into "eternal chains under gloomy darkness [Tartarus]," which is more of a condition of limited powers

(1 Pet. 3:19; 2 Pet. 2:4; Jude 6), **not** so much a place, like a maximum-security prison.–Matt. 28:2; Rev. 22:8.

Archangel

(Gr. *archangelos*) Michael is the only spirit named as an archangel in the Bible. Nevertheless, some Bible scholars believe that 'it is possible that there are other' archangels. However, the prefix "arch," meaning "chief" or "principal," indicates that there is only one archangel, the chief angel. Yes, Gabriel is very powerful, but no Scripture ever refers to him as an archangel. If there were multiple archangels, how could they even be described as an arch (chief or principal) angel? In the Scriptures, "archangel" is never found in the plural. Clearly, Michael is the only archangel and as the highest-ranking angel, like the highest-ranking general in the army, Michael stands directly under the authority of God, as he commands the other angels, including Gabriel, according to the Father's will and purposes. Michael, the Archangel, whose name means, "Who is like God?"); he disputed with Satan over Moses body. (Jude 9) Michael with Gabriel stood guard over the sons of Israel and fought for Israel against demons. (Dan. 10:13, 21) He cast Satan and the demons out of heaven. (Rev. 12:7-9) He will defeat the kings of the earth and their armies at Armageddon, and he will be the one given the privilege of abyssing Satan, the archenemy of God.–Rev. 18:1-2; 19:11-21.

Demon

Throughout history, various religions and cultures have believed in the existence of spirits, whether malevolent, benevolent, or a mix of both. Some dismiss these entities as mere superstitions or products of the imagination. However, the Bible provides insight into their origins and nature.

The Scriptures indicate that God, the Supreme Spirit, created numerous spirit beings. While the Bible acknowledges the existence of wicked spirits, often referred to as demons, it does not suggest that

God created them to be malevolent. So, where did these demons come from?

God created spirit beings with free will, allowing them to choose between good and evil. Regrettably, after humanity's creation, a number of these angels chose rebellion over righteousness.

The initial spirit to revolt became known as Satan, meaning "resister." Overcome with envy and desire for adoration reserved for God, Satan set himself up as a competing deity. Over time, more angels joined Satan, abandoning their divine roles. Prior to Noah's Great Flood, these angels materialized in human forms and interacted directly with humans on earth. (Genesis 6:1-4) Once the Flood commenced, these rebellious angels presumably shed their human forms, returning to the spirit realm and later becoming what we refer to as demons. (Deuteronomy 32:17; Mark 1:34)

When these fallen angels returned to the heavens, they found themselves in a drastically altered circumstance. They were isolated, devoid of their previous privileges. In essence, they were cast into symbolic "pits of dense darkness," estranged from divine enlightenment.

Despite their confinement, these demons maintain significant sway over human thoughts and actions. With Satan at the helm, they are actively "misleading the entire inhabited earth." (Revelation 12:9; 16:14) One of their primary tools for deception is propagating false teachings, often religious, blinding countless individuals from the truth. Some examples include:

- **Life After Death Myth:** Through various deceptive tactics, like apparitions or mysterious voices, demons perpetuate the myth that the dead continue to live and can communicate with the living. This strengthens the false notion of an immortal soul, contrary to the Bible's teaching that "the dead are conscious of nothing at all." (Ecclesiastes 9:5, 6)

- **Relaxed Morality:** Living in a world under the influence of "the wicked one," (1 John 5:19), many are seduced into embracing a lax moral code, where anything goes. The media often glorifies immoral behaviors, making them seem normal, while Biblical principles are ridiculed or deemed outdated.

- **Promotion of Spiritism:** In the Bible, Paul encounters a girl with "a demon of divination." She could predict the future, a gift from her demonic possession. (Acts 16:16) Engaging in or promoting spiritism, which includes activities like astrology or occult practices, is seen as abhorrent in the eyes of God. (Deuteronomy 18:10-12)

Protection against these malevolent entities requires more than mere awareness. The Bible advises: "Subject yourselves . . . to God; but oppose the Devil, and he will flee from you." (James 4:7) Living by Biblical teachings, the only book that exposes the demons and their cunning tactics, fortifies us against their influences. (Ephesians 6:11) We are assured by the Scriptures that wicked spirits and all who defy God will eventually be eradicated, allowing the righteous to live in peace. (Romans 16:20; Proverbs 2:21)

Demon Possession

Demon possession refers to the overwhelming control and influence an unseen wicked spirit has over an individual. In Biblical accounts, victims of demon possession exhibited various symptoms: some lost their speech, some became blind, others displayed erratic behavior, while some showcased unnatural strength. Each one suffered terribly under these unseen tormentors. Both men and women, including children, were not spared. (Mt 9:32; 12:22; 17:15; Mr 5:3-5; Lu 8:29; 9:42; 11:14; Ac 19:16) At times, an individual was oppressed by multiple demons simultaneously, intensifying their torment. (Lu 8:2, 30) However, when the demon was cast out, the affected individual returned to their natural, sane state. It's crucial to note that demon possession is different from common illnesses, as Jesus healed both. (Mt 8:16; 17:18; Mr 1:32, 34)

One of Jesus' notable miracles was liberating those possessed by demons. These wicked spirits had no power against Him. However, not everyone celebrated Jesus' ability to exorcise demons. The Pharisees falsely accused Him of partnering with Beelzebub, the chief demon, when, in fact, Jesus attributed His authority over demons to Jehovah's spirit. (Mt 12:28; Lu 8:39; 11:20) Demons, recognizing Jesus, referred to Him as the "Son of God" and the "Holy One of God." (Mt 8:29; Mr 1:24; 3:11; 5:7; Lu 4:34, 41; Ac 19:15; Jas 2:19) Jesus, however, never allowed them to speak on His behalf. In contrast, a man freed from demonic possession was encouraged to share with others the miracles Jehovah had performed for him. (Mr 5:18-20)

Jesus empowered His twelve apostles and subsequently, a group of seventy disciples, granting them authority over demons. In His name, they could free individuals from demonic influence. (Mt 10:8; Mr 3:15; 6:13; Lu 9:1; 10:17) Even those who weren't directly associated with Jesus or His apostles could expel demons invoking Jesus' name. (Mr 9:38-40; Lu 9:49, 50) After Jesus' death, the apostles maintained this power. When Paul commanded a "demon of divination" to leave a young girl, her masters, who profited from her ability, were infuriated. (Ac 16:16-19) But, when some impostors tried to use the name of "Jesus whom Paul preaches" to cast out demons, they were attacked and humiliated by the demon-possessed man. (Ac 19:13-16)

Nowadays, some mentally disturbed individuals' erratic behaviors may stem from demonic influence. There are claims that spiritual mediums can drive out these demons. However, one must remember Jesus' words: "Many will say to me in that day, 'Lord, Lord, did we not . . . expel demons in your name . . . ?' And yet then I will confess to them: I never knew you!" (Mt 7:22, 23) This highlights the importance of being cautious and vigilant, guarding oneself against the schemes of the Devil and his demons. (1Pe 5:8; Eph 6:11) This underscores the need to "put on the complete suit of armor from God," ensuring protection against the wiles of wicked spirits.

Gehenna

(Gr. *geenna*) (Gehenna) occurs 12 times and is the Greek name for the valley of Hinnom, southwest of Jerusalem (Jer. 7:31), where the horrendous worship of Moloch took place, and it was prophetically said that where dead bodies would be thrown. (Jer. 7:32; 19:6) It was an incinerator where trash and dead bodies were destroyed, not a place to be burned alive or tormented. Jesus and his disciples used Gehenna to symbolize eternal destruction, annihilation, or the "second death," an eternal punishment of death.

Hades

(*hades*) Hades is the standard transliteration into English of the corresponding Greek word haides, which occurs ten times in the UASV. (Matt. 11:23; 16:18; Lu 10:15; 16:23; Ac 2:27, 31; Rev. 1:18; 6:8; 20:13, 14.) It has the underlying meaning of 'a place of the dead, where they are conscious of nothing, awaiting a resurrection, for both the righteous and the unrighteous.' (John 5:28-29; Acts 24:15) It corresponds to "Sheol" in the OT. It does not involve torment and punishment.

Lake of Fire

The Lake of Fire is a biblical symbol representing eternal destruction. It aligns with the term "Gehenna" but stands distinct from "hell," which is often described as the shared grave of humankind.

Is the Lake of Fire Literal? Based on the five references to the "lake of fire" in the Bible, it is understood to be a symbolic representation rather than an actual lake. (Revelation 19:20; 20:10, 14, 15; 21:8). Consider the following that the Bible describes as being cast into the lake of fire:

- **The Devil**: As a spirit, the Devil cannot be physically harmed, so a literal fire wouldn't affect him.
- **The concept of Death**: Death represents a lack of life, not a tangible entity that can be burned.
- **Symbols like "The Wild Beast" and "The False Prophet"**: If these are symbols, it makes sense that the lake they're cast into would also be symbolic.

The Bible equates the lake of fire with the "second death." While the first death, resulting from Adam's sin, can be overturned through resurrection, the "second death" symbolized by the lake of fire represents eternal, irreversible destruction.

Gehenna, mentioned 12 times in the Bible, is another symbol of eternal destruction. While some translations use the term "hell" for Gehenna, it's distinct from the biblical hell.

The term Gehenna comes from the "Valley of Hinnom," located near Jerusalem. Historically, this valley was a site for waste disposal where continuous fires were maintained to burn garbage. This burning valley became a poignant symbol of total annihilation, where fire and worms consumed what was discarded - a place where destruction, not torture, took place.

What About the Eternal Torment? A common question arises from Revelation 20:10, which mentions the Devil, the wild beast, and the false prophet being "tormented day and night forever and ever." Here are reasons this doesn't indicate endless torture:

- The Devil, according to the Bible, will eventually be destroyed.
- Endless life is a gift, not a punishment.
- The "wild beast" and "false prophet" are symbols.
- "Torment" in the Bible can also mean "restraint" or "confinement."

The Greek term for "torment" can also refer to "a state of restraint." This notion of restraint aligns with other biblical uses of the term, linking "torment" with being held or confined. Given this understanding, the Devil's torment in the lake of fire may signify eternal confinement or destruction, not perpetual torture.

Nephilim

The Nephilim were essentially **giant beings**, believed to be the powerful and violent offspring that resulted when wicked angels coupled with human women during Noah's era.

INTRODUCTION TO OLD TESTAMENT TEXTUAL CRITICISM

The term "Nephilim," translated from Hebrew, could mean "The Fellers." It's suggested that this title describes individuals who attacked others with intense aggression and plundered them.

The biblical narrative reveals that the "sons of the true God" were captivated by the beauty of human women. (Genesis 6:2) These "sons of God" weren't humans but spirit beings who defied God's intent. Choosing to abandon their divine realm, they took on human forms and married the women they desired. (Jude 6; Genesis 6:2)

The children born of these unnatural unions weren't regular children. The Nephilim were described as **mighty bullies** and tyrants, renowned for spreading violence and terror. (Genesis 6:4, 6:13) These beings weren't just powerful, but also notorious, labeled as "the mighty ones of old times, the men of fame." (Genesis 6:4)

Interestingly, the Israelite spies, as mentioned in Numbers 13:33, apparently encountered individuals who resembled these legendary Nephilim, even though the original Nephilim had perished long before this encounter. (Genesis 7:21-23)

Debunking Myths About the Nephilim

- **Myth: The Nephilim are still among us today.**

Truth: Jehovah's decision to cleanse the Earth through a global flood eradicated the Nephilim and all other wicked beings. Noah's family, who had Jehovah's favor, were the sole survivors of this cataclysmic event. (Genesis 6:9, 7:12, 13, 23; 2 Peter 2:5)

- **Myth: Humans fathered the Nephilim.**

Truth: The fathers of the Nephilim are described as "sons of the true God" in the scriptures. (Genesis 6:2) The same phrase is often used to denote angels. These angels had the capability to assume human forms. Jude and Peter's writings in the New Testament further emphasize that these angels strayed from their intended positions and responsibilities. (1 Peter 3:19, 20; Jude 6)

- **Myth: The Nephilim were fallen angels themselves.**

Truth: A careful reading of Genesis 6:4 illustrates that the Nephilim were offspring, not the fallen angels themselves. These beings were born from the unions between the materialized angels and human women. As the narrative unfolds, it becomes evident that the creation of the Nephilim was a significant factor leading up to the global flood, as they were the product of the unions that the angels initiated with human women. (Genesis 6:4)

Tartarus

Greek verb *tartaroo* (to "cast into Tartarus") the angels who sinned were cast into the pagan mythological Tartarus, a place of torture or torment. However, in reality, this is not a place; it is a condition, where Satan and his angels are restrained from using some of their former powers, such as materializing in human form.

Sheol

(Heb. *sheol*) Sheol occurs sixty-six times in the UASV. The Greek Septuagint renders Sheol as Hades. It has the underlying meaning of 'a place of the dead, where they are conscious of nothing, awaiting a resurrection, for both the righteous and the unrighteous.' (Gen. 37:35; Psa. 16:10; Ac 2:31; John 5:28-29; Acts 24:15) It corresponds to "Hades" in the NT. It does not involve torment and punishment.

Torment

The term *torment* in the New Testament predominantly originates from the Greek word *ba·sa·ni'zo* and its variants, which appear over 20 times. The root meaning is "to test by the touchstone," which is a *ba'sa·nos*. As the term evolved, it gained the connotation of "examination by applying torture." In the context of the New Testament, the word often conveys the idea of experiencing severe distress or being harassed. It illustrates feelings of profound discomfort or anguish. (Mt 8:29; Lu 8:28; Re 12:2).

Biblical Usage of the Term: The term *ba·sa·ni'zo* appears in diverse scenarios in the Bible:

1. **Physical Affliction**: A manservant's severe paralysis was described as him being "terribly tormented" or enduring severe pain. (Mt 8:6; see also 4:24).

2. **Emotional and Moral Distress**: Lot felt deeply distressed or "tormented in his soul" due to the wicked actions of the Sodomites. (2Pe 2:8).

3. **Challenging Circumstances**: The term was metaphorically used to depict a boat's struggle against the waves. (Mt 14:24; Mr 6:48).

The noun *ba·sa·ni·stes'* found in Matthew 18:34 is sometimes translated as "jailers" or, in other contexts, as "tormentors" or "torturers." Given that torture was a common method to extract information in prisons, this term was occasionally used to describe jailers. Some interpretations of Matthew 18:34 suggest that the very act of imprisonment was a "torment," making "tormentors" synonymous with jailers. The International Standard Bible Encyclopaedia even posits that this term's use in this context might merely refer to jailers. Notably, when Revelation 20:10 mentions the tormented "day and night forever and ever," it could be referring to a perpetual state of constraint. Evidence from Matthew 8:29 and Luke 8:31 supports this notion, where "torment" can also mean "restraint."

Misinterpretations and Clarifications: Some theologians have used the Bible's references to "torment" to advocate for the doctrine of eternal suffering in hellfire. However, a closer examination of Revelation 20:10 suggests a different interpretation. In fact, verse 14 clarifies that "the lake of fire" - the very place where torment takes place - symbolizes "the second death."

Furthermore, while Jesus talks about a rich man entering a "place of torment" (Lu 16:23, 28), he isn't depicting a real person's literal experience. Instead, he presents a parable or illustrative tale. Revelation contains several passages where "torment" is used symbolically, as inferred from the context. (Re 9:5; 11:10; 18:7, 10).